Otto Weibel, Director of Kitchens
The Westin Stamford & Westin Plaza, Singapore

FOOD & WINE
THE WESTIN WAY

WESTIN
HOTELS & RESORTS

Restaurant Haerlin
Hotel Vier Jahreszeiten, Hamburg, Germany

FOOD & WINE
THE WESTIN WAY

BY THE MASTER CHEFS OF
WESTIN HOTELS & RESORTS

WITH
KURT H FISCHER
VICE PRESIDENT • FOOD & BEVERAGE

DESIGNED & COMPILED BY
MERVYN C COLE

EDITED BY
ROSE VONDRASEK
C C TINA LIEW

A BRENDAN INTERNATIONAL PUBLICATION

A BRENDAN WESTIN BOOK

First published with Westin Hotels & Resorts, United States of America in 1994
by Brendan International Publications

Distributor to hotels worldwide
Westin Hotels & Resorts
Corporate Headquarters, 2001 Sixth Avenue, Seattle WA 98121, USA. - Fax: (206) 443 5240

Distributor to the book trade in the United States of America and Canada
Publishers Distribution Service
6893 Sullivan Road, Grawn, Michigan 49637, USA. - Fax: (616) 276 5197

Distributor to the book trade in the United Kingdom and Europe
Gazelle Book Services Limited
Falcon House, Queen Square, Lancaster LA1 1RN, England, UK. - Fax: (0) 524 63232

First Published 1994
ISBN 1-884220-00-2

FOOD & WINE THE WESTIN WAY
is designed & compiled by Mervyn C Cole,
with Kurt H Fischer, Vice President, Food & Beverage, Westin Hotels & Resorts

Published by
Brendan International Publications
with
Westin Hotels & Resorts
Corporate Headquarters, 2001 Sixth Avenue, The Westin Building, Seattle WA 98121
UNITED STATES OF AMERICA

Publisher's Cataloging-in-Publication Data

Food & Wine The Westin Way / by the Master
    Chefs of Westin Hotels & Resorts with Kurt H.
    Fischer ; designed & compiled by Mervyn C.
    Cole. — Seattle, Wash. : Brendan
    International Publications, 1994.

    p. :   col.   ill. ;   cm
    Includes index.
    ISBN: 1-884220-00-2 (hard cover)
    ISBN: 1-884220-01-0 (soft cover)

    1. Cookery, International.   2. Cookery.
I. Fischer, Kurt H.   II. Cole, Mervyn C.,
III. Title: Food and Wine The Westin Way.
TX725.F66   1994   641.59 dc20
    94-73412

Color Separation by Superskill Graphics Pte Ltd
Printed by Singapore National Printers Ltd

DISCLAIMER – Information in this text is believed accurate. However it has been gathered from across four continents, from chefs of many nationalities and therefore information during translation and compilation has been edited, checked many times with every endeavour to avoid error. Any misinformation (or lack of it) is regretted. The authors, compilers & publishers have done whatever possible to ensure accuracy.

Contents

Introduction

by Hiroyoshi Aoki
Chairman & Chief Executive Officer

Westin Hotels & Resorts has experienced many changes in the more than sixty years since its foundation. Despite those changes over the years, a constant priority at Westin has been to serve as leaders in quality within the hospitality industry. One area where Westin most visibly and consistently strives to display this quality is in the food and beverage served to our guests and customers in all our restaurants and fine dining rooms.

Therefore, it is with great pride that I present this first collection of recipes highlighting the great creativity of Westin culinarians from four continents paired with the finest wines from around the world.

Enjoy!

Hiroyoshi Aoki

◀ **THE NEWEST WESTIN HOTEL**
- opened in June 1993
The Westin Osaka,
Osaka, Japan

The Shin Umeda development is now the commercial center of Osaka. The two striking skyscrapers, which are joined at the top, are visible throughout the city, where the architecture has become a symbol of Osaka's future. In the heart of Shin Umeda is the new Westin Osaka, unquestionably the world's finest.

The hotel is one of the most innovative in the world with state-of-the-art features like high-tech room keys, two-line telephones with data ports, and fax capability in every room. Workout in the hotel fitness center or in the swimming pool. Then, for an unforgettable taste of Japan, visit Hanano where tempura, sushi, teppanyaki and sukiyaki rooms surround a formal garden in the hotel.

China – The Westin Way

In May 1992, The Homer Laughlin China Company of Newell, West Virginia — in conjunction with Westin Hotels — revolutionized the foodservice china industry with the introduction of an innovative new product line, the Seattle Collection.

Kurt H Fischer of Westin, together with Homer Laughlin's Director of Design, Jonathan Parry, created the china design to complement a new plating style concept that was under development at the time by Westin. The concept was simple: provide consistent food presentation at every Westin restaurant location.

As an integral part of a sophisticated food presentation, Seattle's shape commands exact positioning at the table and places a clear focus on the food being served. This is achieved through the asymmetrical positioning of the well, subtle rim carvings and a pure cream color. All pieces are completely lead-free.

Established in 1871, The Homer Laughlin China Company is a progressive manufacturer of china products for foodservices and consumer markets worldwide.

THE HOMER LAUGHLIN CHINA CO.

Newell, West Virginia 26050
1-800-452-4462
FAX 304-387-0593

Robert Mondavi & Kurt H. Fischer

Foreword

by Kurt H. Fischer
Vice President, Food & Beverage

"FOOD & WINE THE WESTIN WAY"

There are two reasons why we selected this title.

Obviously, the first reason is that food and wine together form the basis of *the art of dining*. Separately, each one represents an art form, but together they reach their full bloom.

The first cookbook dates back to the time of Emperor Tiberius of Rome (42 BC to 37 AC), but the importance of well-prepared food was evident in wall-paintings and papyrus rolls from Egyptian tombs as early as 2500 BC. Even in those early days, wine was served at important dinners. For the dinner guest, food and wine were always an inseparable pair. However, the two went separate ways to develop from a basic preparation into an elaborate art form.

Originally the ingredients for food items came from the same regions as wine, forming a natural bond. This made food and wine pairing easy. Today, through all kinds of influences and improved transportation, both food and wines can be brought in from all parts of the world to make a perfect dinner. The ability to combine ingredients with different cooking techniques make the culinary arts even more interesting and complete.

The area of wine making has gone through a similar process. While the basic art has not changed, the ingredients have been refined and so has the growing and wine-making process. Today wine makers are much more knowledgeable on which grape variety is best for their soil, how to press their grapes and which process to use to achieve the best quality.

Therefore, we are fortunate to live in a time when *culinary art* and the *art of wine making* are at their prime. All we have to do is to select which combination best suits the occasion, the mood and our palate. Our first food and wine book will give you an opportunity to do so.

"The Westin Way" was selected to highlight what food and wine should achieve together.

Through the centuries, there has been no better place to be hospitable than at a dinner table. At Westin Hotels & Resorts, we provide the best hospitality in the world.

The easiest way to create and solidify a friendship and to show how much you esteem your guest is to serve a beautiful dish and a good glass of wine. This is the way international conflicts are resolved peacefully and many long-lasting friendships are started.

Taking time to enjoy "*Food & Wine The Westin Way*" will provide you and your friends with long-lasting pleasure.

Acknowledgements

by Kurt H Fischer

First of all I would like to say thank you to Mervyn C Cole who initiated this project and provided valuable guidance throughout the various stages of organizing and marketing this book.

Among the many people involved in the production of *"Food & Wine The Westin Way"*, I especially wish to thank Rose Vondrasek for putting together all the recipes and photographs with the assistance of Sandy Parker. Thanks also to Lee Evans for his untiring assistance in finding the various corporate supporters who made the promotions and the production of this book possible.

My sincere thanks go to all the Master Chefs of Westin Hotels & Resorts who participated in these promotions and created these recipes. I am also grateful to the management of The Westin Mission Hills Resort - Rancho Mirage, Walt Disney World Swan - Orlando, The Westin Hotel - Seattle, and Century Plaza Hotel & Tower - Los Angeles, for hosting the different Master Chefs groups to develop the recipes for the various promotions. I also want to thank Mark Knight and Nick Pira of Southern Exposure for photographing all the dishes; Dave Sullivan of The Allied Printers for his good-natured help producing the collateral material for the promotions; Doug Wadden, Professor/Chair of Graphic Design at the University of Washington for organizing the *"Seafood of the World"* design competition, Joe Wells III of The Homer-Laughlin China Company and his team for the production of the "Seattle" Collection China Series.

Thanks are due also to the supporters of our promotions. Without them, our Master Chefs would not have the opportunity to exchange their knowledge and ideas in such a productive way, and our guests and customers would not have the opportunity to sample these dishes. I am also grateful to the Officers and Management teams of all Westin Hotels & Resorts for supporting the promotions and making future ones possible.

In closing, I would like to extend very special thanks to Mr and Mrs Aoki, John Chen and Steve Schnoor. Their continuous support and encouragement to strive to improve quality levels have enabled us to overcome all challenges and to finding satisfaction in solutions.

by Mervyn C Cole

Thank you, Kurt, for giving me the opportunity to be involved in this publication, and for travelling across the continents so many times during the preparation of it, bringing your valued contributions.

I would like to thank all the knowledgeable, helpful and *"stressed-out by me"* people who sometimes worked around the clock to keep up with my demands and schedules; especially to B G Tan for his consistent support.

Also, special thanks to Jeffrey Tan, Mrs Tan, K C, Johnson, Ricky, Richard, Beng Teck, Veera and all the "behind the scene" people. Not forgetting Joyce, Christine, The George-Coshs, The Timmins and The Swinchatts for all their enthusiasm and offer of assistance at all times.

I also want to extend my thanks to everyone else who had contributed to *"Food & Wine The Westin Way"* in any way.

Abbreviations

fl oz	fluid ounce		qt	quart
g	gram		Tbsp	tablespoon
kg	kilogram		tsp	teaspoon
l	liter		cm	centimeter
lb	pound		dl	deciliter
oz	ounce		cl	centiliter
pt	pint			

Conversion Tables

VOLUME

1 centiliter	10 milliliters	0.070 gill
1 deciliter	10 centiliters (100 c.c.)	3.62 fluid ounces
1 deciliter	10 centiliters (100 c.c.)	0.176 pint
1 liter	10 deciliters (1000 c.c.)	1.75980 pints
1 liter	10 deciliters (1000 c.c.)	0.2200 gallon

When cooking fish allow ten minutes of cooking time for each inch of fish thickness. This rule applies except when cooking soups and stews.

Conversion Tables

LIQUID MEASURES - VOLUME

FLUID OUNCES	U.S. MEASURE	IMPERIAL MEASURE	MILLILITERS
	1 tsp	1 tsp	5
$1/4$	2 tsp	1 dessert–spoon	7
$1/2$	1 Tbsp	1 Tbsp	15
1	2 Tbsp	2 Tbsp	28
2	$1/4$ cup	4 Tbsp	56
4	$1/2$ cup or $1/4$ pint		110
5		$1/4$ pint or 1 gill	140
6	$3/4$ cup		170
8	1 cup or $1/2$ pint		225
9			250, $1/4$ liter
10	$1 1/4$ cups	$1/2$ pint	280
12	$1 1/2$ cups or $3/4$ pint		340
15		$3/4$ pint	420
16	2 cups or 1 pint		450
18	$2 1/4$ cups		500, $1/2$ liter
20	$2 1/2$ cups	1 pint	560
24	3 cups or $1 1/2$ pints		675
25		$1 1/4$ pints	700
27	$3 1/2$ cups		750
30	$3 3/4$ cups	$1 1/2$ pints	840
32	4 cups or 2 pints or		900
	1 quart		
35		$1 3/4$ pints	980
36	$4 1/2$ cups		1000, 1 liter
40	5 cups or $2 1/2$ pints	2 pints or 1 quart	1120
48	6 cups or 3 pints		1350
50		$2 1/2$ pints	1400
60	$7 1/2$ cups	3 pints	1680
64	8 cups or 4 pints or 2 quarts		1800
72	9 cups		2000, 2 liters
80	10 cups or 5 pints	4 pints	2250
96	12 cups or 3 quarts		2700
100		5 pints	2800

SOLID MEASURES - WEIGHTS

U.S. AND IMPERIAL MEASURE		METRIC MEASURE	
ounces	pounds	grams	kilos
1		28	
2		56	
$3 1/2$		100	
4	$1/4$	112	
5		140	
6		168	
8	$1/2$	225	
9		250	$1/4$
12	$3/4$	340	
16	1	450	
18		500	$1/2$
20	$1 1/4$	560	
24	$1 1/2$	675	
27		750	$3/4$
28	$1 3/4$	780	
32	2	900	
36	$2 1/4$	1000	1
40	$2 1/2$	1100	
48	3	1350	
54		1500	$1 1/2$
64	4	1800	
72	$4 1/2$	2000	2
80	5	2250	$2 1/4$
90		2500	$2 1/2$
100	6	2800	$2 3/4$

OVEN TEMPERATURE EQUIVALENTS

Fahrenheit	Gas mark	Celsius	Heat of oven
225	$1/4$	107	very cool
250	$1/2$	121	very cool
275	1	·135	cool
300	2	148	cool
325	3	163	moderate
350	4	177	moderate
375	5	190	fairly hot
400	6	204	fairly hot
425	7	218	hot
450	8	232	very hot
475	9	246	very hot

Spring is in the Air

1 Spring is in the Air

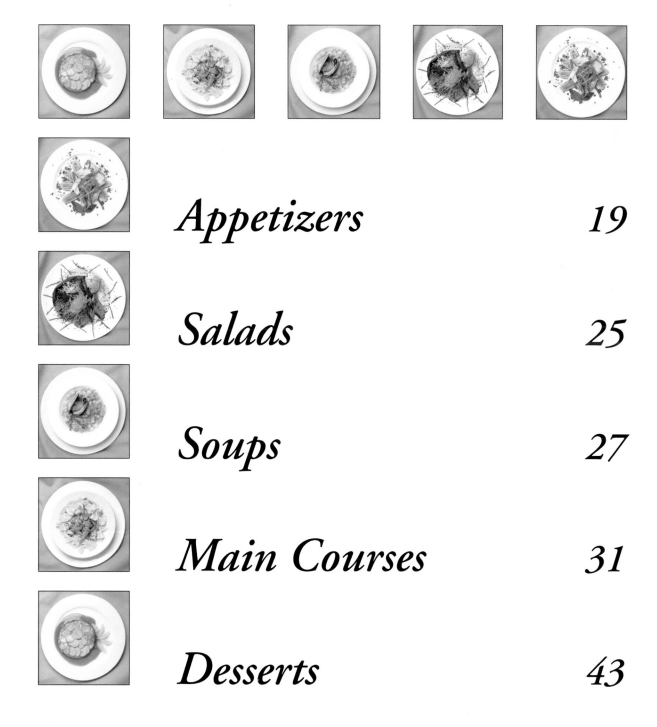

"Spring is in the Air"

Today, we can buy fresh produce all year round; thanks to modern transportation and improved growing methods. However, there is still something special about Spring. Everyone waits for the first Spring blossoms and sprouts of fresh vegetables emerging from the ground.

In our "Spring is in the Air" promotion, fresh produce is combined with other Spring ingredients available and prepared with a selection of ethnic cooking methods.

In the promotion design, the hummingbird feeding from fuschia blossoms highlights the joyous feeling of Spring. The soft colors of the poster reflect the Master Chefs' culinary compositions.

Menu Development Task Force

(from left to right)

Bryan S. Wilson *Winemaker*, Benziger of Glen Ellen

Daniel Simard *Executive Chef*, Westin South Coast Plaza

Patrick Honeywell *Pastry Chef*, Westin South Coast Plaza

Ulrich Ludwig *Executive Chef*, The Westin Mission Hills Resort

Tylun Pang *Executive Chef*, The Westin Kauai

Christoph Leu *Executive Chef*, The Westin Copley Place

Waldo Brun *Corporate Executive Chef*, Walt Disney World Swan

Kurt H. Fischer *Vice President*, Food & Beverage, Westin Hotels & Resorts

"Spring is in the Air"
List of Recipes

Appetizers

Salads

Soups

Main Courses

Desserts

Tylun Pang

Executive Chef
The Westin Kauai, Hawaii

"Fortunate to be Hawaiian born, I have grown up with many cultural influences. This diversity reflects in the style of cooking I enjoy best. The emphasis on using fresh local ingredients adds to a unique cuisine with island flavors. With the help of dedicated farmers and local fishermen it is most rewarding to share the food I grew up with through this regional style of cooking."

- culinary philosophy of Chef Tylun Pang

Chef Tylun Pang of The Westin Kauai, was born and raised in Hawaii. Educated through Westin's Culinary program, Chef Pang has over 18 years of experience at various Westin Hotels and Resorts.

His inventive interpretation of the many cuisines in Hawaii has gained him prestigious culinary awards.

In 1986, Chef Pang was the recipient of The Thurston Dupar Inspirational Award for exemplary service to guests, employees and the Community.

The Westin Kauai, Kauai Lagoons,
Kauai, Hawaii, USA

Yellow Fin Tuna Nicoise

with Balsamic Vinaigrette

Method

Season tuna and sear in hot skillet on all sides, but leave pink in the middle.

Let cool and slice in medallions.

Arrange on plate.

Toss all vegetables with vinaigrette and arrange on plate.

*Balsamic Vinaigrette:
Mix all the ingredients together but add the oil slowly until the mixture thickens slightly.

Season to taste.

Ingredients

Serves 4
4 tsp oil
8 oz tuna
8 oz Haricots verts
8 oz onion, sliced
1 med yellow pepper, julienne
1 med potato, cooked and sliced
3 oz capers
2 Tbsp Parmesan, shaved
6 oz *balsamic vinaigrette
salt, pepper, to taste

*Balsamic Vinaigrette:
4 Tbsp balsamic vinegar
8 Tbsp extra virgin olive oil
1 tsp basil, chopped
salt, freshly ground pepper to taste

Recommended Wines

Benziger 1991 Fumé Blanc

Benziger 1992 Pinot Blanc

Pan Flashed Ahi

with Spicy Miso Vinaigrette

Ingredients

Serves 3
6 oz Ahi (Yellow Fin tuna)

Garnish:
3 oz Daikon, julienne
6 Shiso leaves

Spicy Miso Vinaigrette:
¹/4 cup cider vinegar
2 Tbsp shiro miso (Japanese white bean paste)
1 Tbsp spring onion, chopped
1 Tbsp honey
1 tsp ginger, minced finely
1 tsp sesame oil

Method

Cut Ahi in long rectangular block and sear quickly on all sides so that center remains rare. Dip into iced water and pat dry, cool until ready to slice.

Spicy Miso Vinaigrette:
Mix shiro miso with cider vinegar until smooth. Add the rest of the ingredients and mix well.

Spoon vinaigrette carefully onto platter. Slice the Ahi and arrange in the vinaigrette; garnish with Daikon julienne and Shiso leaves.

Recommended Wines

Benziger 1991 Chardonnay

Benziger 1992 Pinot Blanc

Smoked Tuna

with Grilled Shiitake Mushrooms

Method

For the salad, sauté the mushrooms with the oils, soya sauce, vinegar and garlic. Add the carrots julienne. Add the juice of one lemon.

To serve, place two ounces of sliced smoked tuna on each plate like petals of a flower.

Spoon mushroom salad in center.

Garnish with green onion flower as shown in picture.

Ingredients

Serves 1
4 to 6 Shiitake mushrooms, julienne
3 oz peanut oil
1 tsp dark sesame oil
2 Tbsp soya sauce
3 Tbsp balsamic vinegar
1 tsp minced garlic
1 carrot, peeled, julienne
2 oz fresh smoked tuna

Recommended Wines

Benziger 1992 Pinot Blanc

Benziger 1991 Chardonnay

Oysters Carpaccio
with Vinaigrette

Method

Layer rock salt on the plate, arrange the oyster shells in a circle. Place one leaf of Bibb lettuce in each shell; place one thin slice carpaccio of tenderloin on top; place one oyster in each shell. Top with dash of vinaigrette, sprinkle toasted sesame seeds. Serve.

Vinaigrette:
Whisk all of the ingredients for this together in a bowl.

Ingredients

Serves 4
2 oz lemon with piggy tail
2 doz fresh oysters, shucked (reserve six shells, wash them)
24 small Bibb lettuce leaves
12 oz frozen fillet, thinly sliced
8 tsp toasted sesame seeds
2 lb rock salt

Vinaigrette:
1 Tbsp horseradish
2 Tbsp chopped shallot
1 Tbsp Dijon mustard
4 oz raspberry vinegar
4 oz Vermouth
2 Tbsp salt, pepper, to taste

Recommended Wine

Benziger 1991 Chardonnay

Grilled American Spring Lamb Chop

with Seasonal Mixed Greens & Sun-dried Tomato Vinaigrette

Ingredients

Serves 1
1 single lamb chop, trimmed of fat
1 cup assorted mixed greens: Frisee,
Radiccio, Bibb, watercress (any
seasonal vegetables)
$^1/_8$ head of Savoy cabbage, blanched
$^1/_4$ tomato, peeled
1 oz potato, julienne, fried crisp

Sun-dried Tomato Vinaigrette:
$^1/_2$ cup sun-dried tomato, minced
4 Tbsp Balsamic vinegar
$^3/_4$ cup virgin olive oil
2 cloves of garlic, minced fine
1 Tbsp parsley, chopped
1 Tbsp cracked black pepper
salt, to taste

Method

Brush the lamb chop with olive oil. Grill and season to taste.

While grilling, keep basting the meat to keep from drying up.

Sun-dried Tomato Vinaigrette:
Whisk all ingredients together, adding oil gradually until well blended and thickened. Season to taste.

Arrange all vegetables in a section on plate, then place grilled lamb chops and pour the vinaigrette around.

Recommended Wines
Benziger 1989 Cabernet Sauvignon
Benziger 1989 Merlot

Grilled Breast of Duck Salad

with Szechuan Peppercorn Vinaigrette

Method

Marinate the meat with two tablespoons of dressing before grilling.

Grill duck breast until brown or done.

To prevent meat from drying out, baste with dressing.

Szechuan Peppercorn Vinaigrette:

Whisk all ingredients for the vinaigrette together, adding oils gradually until well blended and thickened.

Season to taste.

Garnish plate with red pepper julienne and black sesame seeds.

Ingredients

Serves 1

5 oz boneless, skinless duck breast

2 whole Shiitake mushrooms

$1/8$ Oriental cabbage, blanched

$1/4$ bunch watercress

3 leaves Bibb lettuce

2 leaves Frisee lettuce

$1/4$ oz carrots, julienne

$1/4$ oz Daikon, julienne

Szechuan Peppercorn Vinaigrette:

1 tsp Szechuan peppercorns, cracked

2 Tbsp rice vinegar

4 Tbsp salad oil

1 tsp sesame oil

1 tsp honey

1 tsp mirin (Japanese sweet sake)

2 Tbsp light soya sauce

$1/2$ Tbsp roasted white sesame seeds

1 Tbsp Chinese parsley, chopped

Recommended Wines

Benziger 1991 Pinot Blanc

Benziger 1989 Merlot

Jicama with Mesclun Salad

and Lime Vinaigrette

Ingredients

Serves 1
3 oz Mesclun
1 Radiccio leaf
4 Jicama, julienne
2 oz red, green, yellow bell peppers, julienne
1 oz carrots, julienne finely
1 1/2 oz *lime vinaigrette

*Lime Vinaigrette:
1 tsp vinegar
2 Tbsp lime juice
1/4 cup olive oil
1 clove garlic, crushed
salt, pepper to taste

Recommended Wine

Benziger 1991 Chardonnay

Method

Mix Jicama with peppers and some of the dressing. Arrange Mesclun around the plate, in the center of the Radiccio leaf, put the Jicama and carrots and peppers julienne.

*Lime Vinaigrette:
Whisk all ingredients together, adding oil gradually until well blended.

Season to taste.

Boston's Light Clam Chowder

Method

Bring white wine and shallots to the boil. Add clams. Boil covered until clams open.

Remove clams and reserve broth.

Remove meat of all large clams and dice. Sauté all vegetables except potatoes.

Add fish stock and clam broth that has been strained. Add potatoes and thyme. Bring to boil and let simmer for ten minutes.

For garnish, use Littleneck clam in shell and parsley.

Ingredients

Serves 3
1 shallot, chopped
9 Quahog clams, washed
3 Littleneck clams, washed
³/₄ cup dry white wine
1 Tbsp oil
2 oz celery, diced
2 oz leeks, diced
2 oz onion, diced
2 oz carrots, diced
2 cloves garlic, chopped
4 oz potatoes, diced
¹/₂ cup fish stock
1 sprig thyme
1 Tbsp parsley, chopped

Recommended Wines

Benziger 1991 Chardonnay

Benziger 1991 Pinot Blanc

Christoph Leu
Executive Chef
The Westin Hotel, Copley Place, Boston

"One needs to have respect for food.
Buy quality products only and treat them as such all the way until they are served.
Use seasonal products whenever possible since they have the best taste. Then enhance its flavor with herbs and spices, rather than mask it.
Let's not forget that we are in charge of serving nutritional, balanced meals at all times."

- culinary philosophy of Chef Christoph Leu

Chef Leu, educated in Switzerland, has spent the last ten years with Westin Hotels & Resorts. He was awarded a silver medal in the 1984 Culinary Exhibition in Calgary, Canada, and a gold medal the following year.

In 1988, he received the Award of Excellence in Food and Beverage of Westin Hotels & Resorts in Kansas City, USA in 1988.

His impressive skills are not only limited to culinary. He speaks no less than four languages, reading and writing at least three.

The Westin Hotel, Copley Place,
Boston, Massachusetts, USA

Mussels with Herbed Broth

and Vegetables

Method

Open mussels in one cup of white wine in a saucepan. Remove mussels, discard shell, reserve liquid. Sauté the eggplant in one tablespoon of butter with the zucchini until half done.

Add basil, tarragon, thyme, garlic, shallots, saffron and liquid from the mussels.

Let boil one minute then add the cream and reduce to soup consistency. Add mussels and diced tomato.

Serve immediately in soup bowls. Garnish with chives.

Ingredients

Serves 3
2 doz fresh large mussels
1 Tbsp basil, thyme, garlic, tarragon, chives
1 pinch saffron
shallot, finely chopped
2 zucchinis, turned
1 medium eggplant, diamond
2 tomatoes, seeded, peeled and diced
3 cups heavy cream
1 cup white wine
2 Tbsp butter

Recommended Wines

Benziger 1991 Chardonnay

Benziger 1992 Pinot Blanc

Skate Wings
and Corn Consommé

Ingredients

Serves 1
1 pint fish stock
2 oz Skate wings, boneless and skinless
1 Tbsp corn, blanched
$^1/_4$ Chinese cabbage, blanched
1 Tbsp red pepper, julienne
1 oz glass noodles, pre-cooked
8 oz chicken consommé
Szechuan pepper, to taste

Method

Place Skate wings in skillet with fish stock and poach for approximately two minutes.

Heat up corn, Chinese cabbage and glass noodles in chicken consommé with Szechuan pepper.

Arrange everything on plate and garnish with julienne of red peppers.

Recommended wines

Benziger 1991 Chardonnay

Benziger 1991 Fumé Blanc

Farfalle Pasta with Shiitake Mushrooms
in Sun-dried Tomato Cream

Method

In a food processor, purée the olive oil, garlic, basil and sun-dried tomatoes.

Bring water to boil in a saucepan to put Farfalle pasta. Sauté the Shiitake mushrooms in some butter. Add cream and let reduce; then add sun-dried tomato mixture. Season with salt and pepper.

Arrange hot pasta in a dish and spoon mushrooms and sauce over pasta.

Ingredients

Serves 1
¹/₂ cup olive oil
1 oz garlic
1 oz basil
6 oz sun-dried tomatoes
2 cups cream
2 oz Shiitake mushrooms, julienne
salt, white pepper
1 order Farfalle pasta
2 oz butter

Recommended Wines
Benziger 1991 Chardonnay
Benziger 1990 Fumé Blanc

Lobster and Eggplant Cannelloni

with Roasted Yellow Sauce

Ingredients

Serves 4
1 large eggplant
2 cloves garlic, chopped
1 ½ tsp fresh rosemary, chopped
2 Tbsp olive oil
1 cup chicken stock
1 Tbsp parsley
3 Tbsp mis de pain
Romano cheese, grated
4 pasta sheets (4 x 5 inch), pre-cooked
2 lobster tails

Yellow Pepper coulis:
2 yellow peppers
1 Tbsp olive oil
1 clove garlic, chopped
2 shallots, chopped.
½ cup white wine
thyme

Method

Cut eggplant in half and score meat side. Sprinkle with salt and let sit for half hour.

Bake on oiled sheet pan for half an hour at 350 degrees Fahrenheit.

Remove skin and take out seeds.

Sauté garlic in olive oil. Add eggplant, chicken stock and rosemary. Reduce to thick paste.

Purée in food processor with yellow pepper coulis. Bake for ten minutes.

Cook lobster tails. Cut in half and arrange on plate with sauce and sliced cannelloni.

Yellow Pepper coulis:
Roast peppers in 400 degrees Fahrenheit oven until skin turns brown. Peel and remove seeds.

Sauté garlic and shallots. Add wine and peppers. Purée in food processor.

Recommended Wine

Benziger 1991 Chardonnay

Grilled Pancetta-Wrapped Prawns

with Fennel Cream Sauce

Method

Fennel Cream Sauce:

Sauté shallots in one ounce butter until translucent. Deglaze with white wine and reduce by half. Add cream and reduce by half more. Blanch fennel in boiling water for five minutes and cool in an ice bath. Coarsely slice and purée in blender until smooth consistency. Add to cream reduction mixture just before serving and add salt and pepper to taste.

Grilled Shrimp:

Wrap one slice of pancetta around each shrimp. Grill for five to six minutes on each side or until pancetta is crispy and shrimp bright pink.

Blanch Kale in boiling water and cool in ice bath. Arrange three well drained leaves per plate with stems meeting center and place one shrimp on each leaf with tail to center. Drizzle one ounce of sauce on each plate.

Ingredients

Serves 6

1 small head purple Kale
18 shrimp, peeled, deveined, with tail on
9 oz pancetta, sliced in $^1/_2$ oz portions
1 head fennel
10 oz heavy cream
$^1/_4$ cup Benziger Fumé Blanc
2 shallots, finely chopped
3 oz butter

Recommended Wine

Benziger 1991 Fumé Blanc

Chef Keller Award

Ulrich Ludwig
Executive Chef
The Westin Mission Hills Resort, Rancho Mirage

*The Westin Mission Hills Resort,
Rancho Mirage, California, USA*

"A Chef's ego has no place in the kitchen."
"The best culinary products are not necessarily the most expensive or complicated in presentation."
"Sharing recipes are just as important as creating them."
"My culinary staff are like seeds in a garden. First I plant them with my expectations, then I nurture them with my encouragement and respect. Then I cultivate them with education and guidance. Last but not least, I watch them blossom with my congratulations."

- culinary philisophy of Chef Ulrich Ludwig

As Executive Chef, Mr Ludwig has established a reputation as one of Palm Springs' most talented chefs. He has devoted much time to creating innovative menus and catering to a select clientele of Palm Springs celebrities.

Chef Ludwig has been a member of Westin's executive food and beverage staff for more than a decade. He held the position of Executive Chef at The Westin Hotel, Ottawa, where he served the former Prime Minister, Pierre Trudeau, as well as Russian dignitaries and English royalty.

In 1990, he was honored with Westin's Chef Keller Award for creative cuisine and his dining facilities were named Best Food and Beverage Operations of Westin in Canada.

Roasted Monkfish
and Lobster Spring Rolls

Method

Butterfly the monkfish and pound slightly. Roll up with Chinese cabbage leaves. Coat with bacon slices. Secure with toothpicks. Roast fish in hot skillet and place in oven at 400 degrees Fahrenheit for fifteen minutes. Remove and keep warm. Deglaze monkfish and arrange on lobster sauce.

Lobster Spring Rolls:
Sauté garlic, lobster, Chinese cabbage, Shiitake mushrooms, diced red and yellow peppers in sesame oil and ginger and add scallions. Let cool and wrap in spring roll wrappers and deep fry.

Ingredients

Serves 2
12 oz monkfish, cleaned
6 slices bacon
2 leaves Chinese cabbage, blanched
$^3/_4$ Tbsp brandy
$^1/_2$ cup lobster stock
$^1/_2$ cup cream
coriander, to taste

Lobster Spring Rolls:
3 oz lobster, diced
1 oz Chinese cabbage, diced
$^1/_2$ oz Shiitake mushrooms, diced
$^1/_2$ oz red pepper
$^1/_2$ Tbsp scallions
1 glove garlic, chopped
$^1/_4$ tsp ginger, chopped
1 tsp sesame oil
2 spring roll wrappers, 8 inch square

Recommended Wines

Benziger 1991 Chardonnay

Benziger 1991 Pinot Blanc

Ginger Steamed Onaga

with Oriental Sausages

Ingredients

Serves 1

12 oz fillet of Onaga (red snapper), skin on

2 oz Chinese sausage

1 whole fresh Shiitake mushroom

2 oz fresh ginger, peeled, julienne

½ head of Chinese cabbage

4 Tbsp light soya sauce

4 Tbsp peanut oil

2 oz onion slices

Method

Arrange in deep soup plate, with the fish fillet first. Arrange the mushroom, Chinese sausage slices and sprinkle with ginger julienne.

Put in a steamer and steam until done.

Pour soya sauce over fish.

Heat peanut oil until smoking, fry onion slices. Also drizzle a little peanut oil over fish just before serving.

Garnish with fried onion slices and Chinese parsley strips.

Recommended Wines

Benziger 1991 Chardonnay

Benziger 1991 Fumé Blanc

Roulade of Chicken
with Smoked Salmon, Sun-dried Tomatoes & Capers

Method

Lay chicken breast flat with skin side down, place spinach leaves flat in the middle of breast and put sliced salmon in center. Place spinach leaves over salmon and roll chicken lightly. Season with salt, pepper and fresh thyme, drizzle with olive oil and bake.

for Sun-dried Tomato Sauce:
Heat sauté pan with olive oil, sauté shallots, capers and sun-dried tomatoes, add lemon juice, and white wine, let reduce by half.

Lower heat and whisk in whole butter; add chopped parsley, salt and pepper.

Ingredients

Serves 2
1 each 8 oz boneless chicken breast
$^1/_2$ oz fresh spinach leaves, sauteed
$^1/_2$ oz smoked salmon, sliced
$^1/_4$ tsp fresh thyme
salt, pepper
olive oil

for Sun-dried Tomato Sauce:
olive oil
juice of one lemon
$^1/_4$ oz capers
1 shallot, minced
1 oz sun-dried tomatoes
$^1/_4$ cup white wine
2 Tbsp whole unsalted butter
salt, pepper
1 tsp parsley, chopped

Recommended Wines

Benziger 1991 Fumé Blanc

Benziger 1991 Pinot Blanc

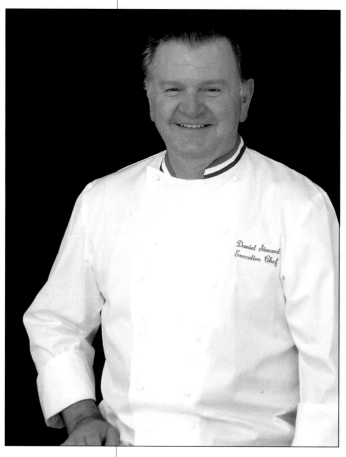

Daniel Simard
Executive Chef
The Westin Hotel, Los Angeles Airport

*The Westin Hotel, Los Angeles Airport,
Los Angeles, California, USA*

"Food these days is that it should be fresh and healthy".

- culinary philosophy of Chef Daniel Simard

Daniel Simard was born in Dijon Burgundy, a province of France. After completing his three years apprenticeship in Beaune, he went to put his culinary talent to test in the South of France.

Being an adventurous person, Chef Simard left France to work in Africa. During this stint, he became very well-known and was enticed to join Westin Hotels & Resorts. His first job with Westin was at the Philippine Plaza Hotel in the Philippines. Later he spent five years at the Century Plaza Hotel as Chef de Cuisine and has been with Westin Hotels & Resorts since.

His culinary expertise is worldwide. He is versatile and loves to be one step ahead of the times.

Medallions of Veal
with Trio of Mushrooms, Lime Leaf Butter

Method

Sauté veal medallions, remove from pan and add mushrooms. Cook until tender. Remove from pan, then add chopped shallots and only two of the lime leaves, chopped. Deglaze with wine, add veal stock and reduce. Finish sauce with two tablespoons of butter and strain. Arrange mushrooms in the center of the plate, between the medallions.

Place lime leaf butter around items and garnish with two whole lime leaves.

Ingredients

Serves 2
5 oz veal loin, trimmed and cut into two medallions
1 piece oyster mushroom, cut in half
1 Shiitake mushroom, cut in half
1 button mushroom, cut in half

for sauce:
4 pieces lime leaves
1 Tbsp shallots, chopped
2 Tbsp butter
1 oz white wine
1 oz veal stock
salt, pepper to taste

Recommended Wines

Benziger 1991 Pinot Blanc

Benziger 1991 Fumé Blanc

Honey & Herb Glazed American Lamb Loin

on Braised Horenso Spinach

Ingredients

Serves 1
1 lamb loin, trimmed of fat and bones

for glaze:
1 Tbsp honey
1 Tbsp Dijon mustard
1 tsp thyme
1 tsp rosemary
2 tsp parsley, chopped
salt, pepper
1 tsp garlic, chopped

for vegetables:
1 bunch Horenso spinach, cleaned
2 cloves garlic, sliced
3 oz lamb jus
2 Tbsp butter

for garnish:
1 oz sweet potato, julienne, deep fried

Method

Heat butter, add garlic slices and sauté. Add spinach, lamb jus and braise with cover until spinach is wilted. Season the lamb loin and sear in hot sauté pan. Remove from the pan and place on cooking rack.

Spread honey and herb glaze evenly over lamb and roast for 12 to 15 minutes. Slice and arrange with braised spinach.

Serve with sliced lamb.

Recommended Wines

Benziger 1989 Cabernet Sauvignon

Benziger 1989 Merlot

American Spring Lamb Loin
en Ficelle

Method

Blanch cabbage leaves briefly. Butterfly lamb loin and pound slightly. Roll Savoy cabbage and lamb loin in cheese cloth and tie securely. Boil potatoes. Heat up beef consommé and add remaining vegetables. Bring to boil and add lamb. Let simmer for ten minutes, or until medium rare.

Place vegetables and broth in bowl and arrange sliced lamb loin on top.

Serve with condiments.

Ingredients

Serves 2
12 oz lamb loin
4 Savoy cabbage leaves, large
4 small potatoes
8 baby carrots
3 oz turnips, diced
1 oz celery, diced
1 ¹/₂ oz leeks, diced
12 oz beef consommé
1 sprig thyme

for Condiments:
2 oz Dijon mustard
2 oz cornichons
2 oz onions

Recommended Wines

Benziger 1989 Merlot

Benziger 1991 Pinot Noir

Roast Tenderloin

with Sea Scallops on Potato "Tian"

Ingredients

Serves 1
6 oz roast tenderloin
2 oz sea scallops
5 oz vegetables, diced: carrots, yellow squash, zucchini, turnip
4 asparagus tips
1 potato, sliced
2 oz butter
2 oz Madiera sauce

Method

Sauté the potato in butter until cooked. Blanch all vegetables and asparagus and sauté in butter. Burn off scallops on the broiler.

Use rosemary branch for skewer.

In center of plate, arrange the potato in small circle. Next, place all the vegetables and asparagus around the plate. On top of the potato, pour sauce and place the roasted fillet and the skewered sea scallops as in picture.

Recommended Wines

Benziger 1989 Merlot

Benziger 1992 Pinot Blanc

Hot Banana Tartlette

with Creole Sauce

Method

Roll pâte sucré to an eighth inch thick and cut out six-inch rounds.

Make a caramel, stop cooking with water, cool until syrupy. Add four bananas cut into one eighth inch slices. Let marinate.

Ginger Confit:

Cook minced ginger in a simple syrup. Cool. On a buttered and floured sheet pan, arrange dough circles, sprinkle with confit, and arrange bananas, overlapping in a circle towards the center. Sprinkle with more ginger and bake 15 minutes at 400 degrees Fahrenheit.

Place on serving dish, and pour sauce around. Garnish with lime zests and lime wedges.

Creole Sauce:

Press the apricot glaze, dark rum and Cream Fraiche and two bananas in cuisinart until smooth. Pour in hot caramel. Process until smooth. Cool.

Ingredients

Serves 4
18 oz sugar, caramelized
6 bananas, ripe
18 oz Creme Fraiche
1 ½ oz dark rum
4 oz apricot glaze, melted
ginger
lime

Recommended Wines

Benziger 1988 Blanc de Blancs

Benziger 1991 Muscat Canelli

Enjoy the perfect complement
to every meal with the fine coffees from
General Foods
at
Westin Hotels & Resorts

Banana Mousseline

with Cointreau

Method

Melt the white chocolate in a bowl. Soften the gelatin sheets in water. Warm the Cointreau and add gelatin sheets to it. Mix the Cointreau into the banana purée.

Take approximately one fifth of the soft whipped cream and whip it into the melted white chocolate to a smooth consistency. Add the banana-Cointreau mixture. Fold in the remaining whipped cream. Spread onto a sheet pan to a height of one inch. Freeze.

Cut into "petal" shapes, top with fresh sliced bananas which have been brushed with apricot glaze.

Present as shown.

Ingredients

Serves 10
2 ¹/₂ lb white chocolate
2 qt soft whipped cream
1 lb fresh pureed banana
5 sheets gelatin
¹/₂ cup Cointreau
chocolate sauce
vanilla sauce
6 fresh sliced bananas
apricot glaze

Recommended Wines

Benziger 1988 Blanc de Blancs

Benziger 1991 Muscat Canelli

Poached Pear

in Cointreau Cream

Ingredients

Serves 12
12 small pears
2 cups white wine
2 cups water
1 lb granulated sugar
1 cinnamon stick
¹/₂ lemon, cut in wedge

for Cointreau Cream:
1 qt cream
1 lb 6 oz pastry cream
5 sheets gelatin
¹/₄ cup Cointreau

for Garnish:
36 oz raspberry or strawberry coulis

Recommended Wines

Benziger 1991 Muscat Canelli

Benziger 1988 Blanc de Blancs

Method

Poach the pears in the wine, water, sugar, cinnamon and lemon mixture. Reserve the pears and store in refrigerator.

Whip the cream until stiff. Fold into pastry cream. Soften the gelatin in cold water. Warm Cointreau and add the gelatin until dissolved. Transfer one third of the cream mixture into small rings and place one pear into the middle of each and refrigerate until firm.

Present as shown with raspberry or strawberry coulis.

Triple Chocolate Terrine

Method

Combine the sugar, egg yolks and whole eggs in a mixing bowl. Set the bowl over simmering water and heat mixture to 110 degrees Fahrenheit, stirring constantly. Remove from heat and whip to sabayon consistency. Whip the cream, then fold in egg mixture. Divide into three one-pound parts. Reserve.

for the filling:

Take the melted milk chocolate and stir into the base. Soften the gelatin in cold water, then dissolve in the Cointreau which has been warmed over the stove. Quickly mix the gelatin and Cointreau into a small part of the chocolate mixture, then stir in the remaining mix.

Follow this same procedure for the white and dark chocolate fillings. Take a small round terrine and fill with the three chocolate fillings. Freeze for two hours. Un-mould and top with white chocolate. Chill and serve with blackberry and raspberry coulis as shown.

Recommended Wines

Benziger 1989 Merlot

Benziger 1991 Muscat Canelli

Ingredients

Serves 10
6 oz granulated sugar
10 egg yolks
2 eggs
2 $^1/_2$ cups cream
Milk Chocolate filling:
10 oz melted milk chocolate
$^1/_3$ of filling base
1 gelatin sheet
2 Tbsp Cointreau
White Chocolate filling:
10 oz melted white chocolate
$^1/_3$ of filling base
1 gelatin sheet
2 Tbsp Cointreau
Dark Chocolate filling:
10 oz melted dark chocolate
$^1/_3$ of filling base
1 gelatin sheet
2 Tbsp Cointreau
20 oz blackberry or strawberry coulis

2 España

"España"

*Spain is a country rich in tradition and the arts.
The church in the design represents tradition, the Flamenco dances, the arts and the
ships represent the historic importance of Spain.
The ships are also home of the seafarers who brought back to Spain many exotic spices
and ingredients.
Thanks to those influences, Spain's cuisine has become internationally renowned and we
are very proud to present a small selection of those world famous dishes.*

Menu Development Task Force

(from left to right)

Kenny Chei *Apprentice,* Walt Disney World Swan

Edward Gee *Assistant Pastry Chef,* Walt Disney World Swan

Menze Heroian *Director, Food & Beverage,* Walt Disney World Swan

Richard Carpenter *Executive Pastry Chef,* Walt Disney World Swan

Jose Ramon *Executive Chef,* El Dorado Petit Restaurant, New York

Kurt H. Fischer *Vice President, Food & Beverage,* Westin Hotels & Resorts

Waldo Brun *Corporate Executive Chef,* Walt Disney World Swan

David S. Milligan *Vice President, Prestige Accounts,* The House of Seagram

Carlos Cancho *Sous Chef,* Walt Disney World Swan

Kimberley Storey *Apprentice,* Walt Disney World Swan

"España"
List of Recipes

Waldo Brun

Corporate Executive Chef
Walt Disney World Swan, Orlando

"I believe in cooking fresh foods from the finest ingredients, attainable, authentically and simply prepared with great taste and flavor. I love to cook!"

- culinary philosophy of Chef Waldo Brun

Born in Switzerland, he has been Executive Chef of Westin Hotels & Resorts for 28 years.

*Walt Disney World Swan,
Orlando (Walt Disney World), Florida, USA*

Croquetas De Pollo

(Chicken Croquettes)

Method

Make a thick bechamel with milk and roux, add chicken, ham and egg.

Season to taste, pour into oiled pan and refrigerate overnight.

Shape croquettes, bread and deep fry until golden brown.

Garnish with tomato concasse.

Ingredients

Makes 12 croquettes
1 pint milk
roux
4 oz chicken breast, boiled and chopped
1 Tbsp cooked ham, chopped
1 Tbsp Serrano ham, chopped
1 Tbsp hard boiled egg, chopped
1 pinch nutmeg
salt, pepper
flour, egg wash
breadcrumbs for breading
tomato concasse for garnish

Recommended Wines

Torres Vina Sol

Torres Gran Vina Sol

Conejo Al Ajillo
(Rabbit with Garlic)

Ingredients

Serves 1
4 oz rabbit meat, diced
2 oz virgin olive oil
2 garlic cloves, chopped
¹/₂ tsp dry red chilli pepper, sliced
salt, pepper
parsley, chopped

Method

Sauté rabbit in olive oil, add garlic and chilli peppers; sauté for about three minutes.

Season with salt and pepper to taste.

Sprinkle chopped parsley and serve very hot.

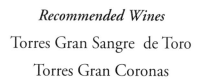

Recommended Wines

Torres Gran Sangre de Toro

Torres Gran Coronas

Gambas Al Ajillo

(Garlic Shrimp)

Method

Peel and devein shrimp. Dry the shrimp well and season with salt.

Heat oil in six-inch casserole and add in this order: Garlic, shrimp and chilli pepper.

Sauté quickly for about two minutes or until shrimp are done.

Sprinkle chopped parsley on and serve piping hot.

Ingredients

Serves 1
6 jumbo shrimp
2 oz extra virgin olive oil
2 each garlic cloves, sliced
¹/₂ tsp dry red chilli pepper, sliced
salt to taste
parsley, chopped

Recommended Wines

Torres Gran Vina Sol

Torres Gran Sangre de Toro

Kokotxas Al Ajillo

(Red Snapper Kokotxas with Garlic)

Ingredients

Serves 1
4 oz Kokotxas of red snapper
2 oz virgin olive oil
2 garlic cloves, chopped
$^1/_2$ tsp dry red chilli pepper, sliced
salt, pepper
parsley, chopped

Note: Kokotxas are small tender parts found under the head of the fish.

Method

Sauté Kokotxas in olive oil, add garlic and chilli pepper, sauté for about one minute.

Check to ensure seasoning is to taste.

Sprinkle chopped parsley and serve very hot.

Recommended Wine

Torres Gran Vina Sol

Rollitos de Ternera con Aceitunas

(Veal Rolls with Black Olives)

Method

Season scallopini with salt and pepper, fill with spinach and red pepper; roll and flour. In saucepan, sauté scallopini in oil until brown, add onion, garlic and tomatoes. Cook for two minutes. Add wine and veal stock. Braise veal in sauce for ten minutes. Remove and reduce sauce.

Arrange veal rolls on serving plate. Strain sauce and pour over veal.

Garnish with black olives.

Ingredients

Serves 1
2 veal scallopini, 3 oz each
6 spinach leaves, blanched
1 small red pepper, roasted, peeled, seeded
2 oz olive oil
1 Tbsp onion, chopped
1 tsp garlic, chopped
1 small tomato, peeled, seeded, chopped
1/4 cup dry white wine
1 cup veal stock
6 black olives
flour, for dusting
salt, pepper

Recommended Wines

Torres Gran Coronas

Torres Gran Sangre de Toro

Gazpacho Andaluz

(Gaspacho)

Method

Coarsely cut all vegetables and bread, combine all ingredients, cover and marinate with the rest of ingredients overnight.

Place ingredients in electric blender and purée, strain through sieve.

Adjust seasoning and color. Soup should be reddish, add tomato paste if necessary.

Serve very cold.

Offer garnish separately.

Recommended Wines

Torres Vina Sol

Torres Gran Vina Sol

Ingredients

Serves 6 - 8

2 medium cucumbers, peeled and seeded

8 medium ripe tomatoes

1 small onion (optional)

1 medium green pepper, seeded

2 garlic cloves

2 ¹/₂ oz French bread

4 cups cold water

¹/₄ cup red wine vinegar

4 Tbsp olive oil

salt, to taste

6 oz tomato paste (optional)

Garnish:

1 cup white bread without crust, diced

1 cup onion, diced (optional)

1 cup green pepper, diced

1 cup tomatoes, peeled, seeded, diced

1 cup cucumbers, peeled, seeded, diced

Pollo con Langosta

(Chicken with Lobster)

Ingredients

Serves 1
2 oz olive oil
1 each 4 oz half chicken breast, boned and skinned
1 each 1 lb live Maine lobster
1 Tbsp garlic, chopped
1 Tbsp onion, chopped
1 tsp medium tomato, peeled, seeded, diced
1 cup dry white wine
few drops Pernod
$^1/_2$ oz chocolate, shredded
4 each almonds, toasted
roux
salt, pepper

Method

Boil lobster in salted water for about ten minutes. Remove lobster and reserve the water to make a strong lobster stock.

Remove shell from lobster and add to lobster stock.

In saucepan, heat oil, add garlic, onion and chicken.

Sauté for about two minutes and add tomato, white wine, chocolate, almonds and lobster stock.

Cook over moderate heat for about ten minutes until chicken is done.

Remove chicken and thicken the sauce with roux. Season sauce with salt and pepper, Pernod.

Arrange chicken and lobster on serving dish and pour sauce over.

Recommended Wines

Torres Gran Coronas Mas La Plana

Torres Gran Vina Sol

Pato con Peras

(Duck with Pears)

Method

In a saucepan, heat olive oil. Add duck legs and brown on both sides.

Add mirepoix and cook for two minutes. Add sherry and duck stock, cover and bake in the oven for about 30 minutes or until legs are tender.

Remove duck legs and thicken the sauce with some roux. Adjust seasoning and strain through fine china cap.

Arrange duck legs on serving plate and pour sauce over. Garnish with one whole pear and balls of other pear.

Ingredients

Serves 1
2 duck legs, skinless
2 oz olive oil
1 cup mirepoix (diced carrots, celery, onion, tomato, bay leaf and fresh herbs)
1 cup dry sherry
16 oz duck stock
roux
2 large pears, poached
salt, pepper

Recommended Wines

Torres Gran Coronas Mas La Plana

Torres Gran Coronas

Paloma con Lentejas y Chorizo

(Squab with Lentil & Chorizo Sausage)

Ingredients

Serves 1
1 small squab
8 oz lentil
1 tsp garlic
$^1/_2$ cup carrots, diced
1 bay leaf
6 oz demi-glaze
6 oz water
4 oz chorizo sausage
2 oz olive oil
1 sprig of fresh rosemary
1 sprig of fresh thyme
salt, pepper

Method

Season squab with salt and pepper, put fresh herbs inside the bird. Roast in moderate oven for 30 minutes or until tender. Let cook and remove all bones.

In the meantime, put the lentil in saucepan with the water, demi-glaze, carrots, garlic and bay leaf.

Cook for one hour or until done.

Slice chorizo and fry in olive oil.

Pour lentils in serving dish and arrange squab and chorizo on top.

Recommended Wines

Torres Gran Coronas Mas La Plana

Torres Gran Coronas

Bacalao con Sanfaina y Musolina de Ajos Tiernos

(Codfish Baked with Vegetables & Garlic Mousseline)

Method

In a skillet, heat half of the oil and add half of the garlic and the vegetables julienne. Sauté, season with salt and pepper. Set aside.

Sauté fish with rest of the oil. Mix mayonnaise with rest of garlic.

In a casserole dish, arrange fish and put vegetables on top.

Cover and bake in the oven for about ten minutes. Pour mayonnaise/garlic mixture on top, just before serving.

Ingredients

Serves 1

1 codfish fillet, 8 oz
1/2 cup onion, julienne
1/2 cup red pepper, julienne
1/2 cup eggplant, julienne
1/2 cup zucchini, julienne
1 small tomato, peeled, seeded, julienne
2 tsp garlic, chopped
4 oz olive oil
1/2 cup mayonnaise
salt, pepper

Recommended Wines

Torres Gran Vina Sol

Torres Vina Sol

Richard Carpenter
Executive Pastry Chef
Walt Disney World Swan, Orlando

"I believe in fun with food. I enjoy the challenge of providing our guests with a daily show from our display Pastry Shop. We are constantly on stage with an audience."

- culinary philosophy of Chef Richard Carpenter

Chef Carpenter graduated from the Culinary Institute of America.

Walt Disney World Swan,
Orlando (Walt Disney World), Florida, USA

Rape en Salsa Verde
(Monkfish Basque Style)

Method

Heat oil in heavy skillet. Season monkfish with salt and pepper, flour lightly. Sauté for two minutes.

Do not let it brown, add garlic, onion and asparagus. Cook for one minute.

Add flour and cook for another minute.

Add white wine and fish stock.

Bring to a boil and adjust seasoning, add green peas and chopped parsley.

Next, add clams, mussels and shrimp.

Cover and cook over moderate heat for 20 minutes or until monkfish is done.

Ingredients

Serves 1
2 monkfish fillets, 4 oz each
2 clams
2 mussels
2 jumbo shrimp
2 white asparagus
$1/4$ cup green peas
2 oz olive oil
1 Tbsp onion, chopped
1 tsp garlic, chopped
1 tsp flour
3 oz white wine
6 oz fish stock
1 Tbsp parsley, chopped
salt, pepper

Recommended Wines
Torres Gran Vina Sol

Torres Vina Sol

Pescado a la Sal con Salsa Romesco y Vegetales al Vapor

(Snapper Baked in Salt with Romesco Sauce & Steamed Vegetables)

Ingredients

Serves 2
1 each 2 lb whole red snapper
4 lb salt
10 oz water
2 oz *Romesco sauce
2 oz olive oil
1 sprig of rosemary
3 oz mixed vegetables, steamed

*Romesco Sauce:
$^1/_2$ cup almonds, toasted
2 cloves garlic, roasted
2 sliced French bread, fried
2 tomatoes, peeled, seeded, roasted
1 red bell pepper, roasted
$^1/_2$ cup red wine vinegar
1 cup olive oil
salt, to taste
cayenne pepper

Method

Mix salt and water. **In baking dish, put salt and red snapper, making sure fish is completely enclosed with salt. Bake in 400 degrees Fahrenheit oven for about 20 minutes.

Remove fish from salt and fillet. Serve with *Romesco sauce, olive oil with rosemary and steamed vegetables.

Romesco Sauce:

Put all ingredients except oil, in electric blender. Blend to purée, gradually add oil as in making of mayonnaise and season with cayenne pepper.

** Fish covered in salt.

Recommended Wines

Torres Gran Vina Sol

Torres Vina Sol

Calamares Rellenos en Su Tinta

(Stuffed Squid with Ink Sauce)

Method

Clean squid, chop tentacles and head, mix with pork meat.

In large saucepan, heat olive oil and add garlic, onion, carrot and parsley.

Add pork meat and chopped squid tentacles mix, white bread and half of pinenuts. Season with salt and pepper; cook until meat is done. Cool.

Fill the squids and place on oiled baking dish. Bake in moderate oven for 20 minutes.

In the meantime, add the wine, stock and ink to the saucepan and reduce by half. In electric blender mix the almonds, rest of pinenuts, chocolate and French bread to purée.

Add some fish stock if necessary to obtain a thick paste. Add this paste to reduced stock. Heat it again and adjust seasoning.

Pour over stuffed squids and serve. Garnish with green peas.

Recommended Wines

Torres Gran Vina Sol

Torres Sangre de Toro

Ingredients

Serves 4
1 lb squid, cleaned
10 oz pork meat, ground
1 small onion, diced
1 small carrot, diced
1 Tbsp garlic, chopped
1 tsp parsley, chopped
olive oil
3 oz white bread
4 oz pinenuts, toasted
10 oz fish stock
6 oz dry white wine
10 almonds, toasted
1 oz chocolate, shredded
2 sliced French bread, fried
2 oz squid ink
2 oz green peas
salt, pepper

Gran Zarzuela

(Zarzuela)

Ingredients

Serves 1

1 snapper fillet, 3 oz
1 monkfish, 3 oz
1 grouper fillet, 3 oz
2 clams
2 mussels
2 jumbo shrimp
2 oz lobster tail
1 oz squid rings
2 oz olive oil
1 Tbsp onion, chopped
1 tsp garlic, chopped
1 tomato, peeled, seeded, chopped
1 Tbsp flour
1 oz Spanish brandy
2 oz dry white wine
8 oz lobster and fish stock
1 pinch saffron
1 tsp parsley, chopped
1 bay leaf
salt, pepper
2 heart shaped croutons

Method

Heat oil in casserole. Lightly flour all fish and sauté. Add garlic, onion and flour. Cook for two minutes. Add Spanish brandy and flame. Add white wine, lobster and fish stock and tomato. Bring sauce to a boil, then add bay leaf and saffron.

Adjust seasoning with salt and pepper.

Next, add the seafood in this order:

Lobster, clams, shrimp, mussels and squids.

Cover and cook until done (15 to 20 minutes). Sprinkle with chopped parsley and garnish with heart shaped croutons.

Recommended Wines

Torres Gran Coronas

Torres Gran Vina Sol

Fidevada
(Noodles Baked with Seafood)

Method

Deep fry pasta until golden brown.

In earthenware casserole, heat oil and add garlic, onion and tomato. Cook for about two minutes.

Add wine and lobster fish stock. Bring to boil.

Add deep fried pasta and seafood.

Bake in oven for about 20 minutes or until pasta is soft.

Season to taste.

TORRES

FOUNDED 1870

Viña Sol

ESTATE BOTTLED

MIGUEL TORRES, S.A. • VILAFRANCA DEL PENEDÈS • PRODUCT OF SPAIN
ALC. 10.5% BY VOL. • WHITE TABLE WINE • 750 ML.   PENEDES

Ingredients

Serves 1

3 oz Angel hair pasta, broken in three parts

3 oz lobster tail

3 clams

3 jumbo shrimp

3 oz sea scallops

2 oz squid rings

2 oz olive oil

1 tsp garlic, chopped

1 tsp onion, chopped

1 small tomato, peeled, seeded, chopped

¼ cup dry white wine

8 oz lobster and fish stock

salt, pepper

Recommended Wines
Torres Vina Sol

Torres Sangre de Toro

Paella Parellada

(Off the Shell Seafood Paella)

Method

In paella pan, heat oil and add garlic, onion and tomato. Cook for two minutes. Add squid, wine and reduce. Add rice and lobster stock. Bring to a boil and season with salt and pepper.

Then add the rest of the seafood and the saffron. Place in moderate oven and cook for about 15 to 20 minutes. Just before rice is done, arrange asparagus, peas and pimientos on top.

Remove from oven and let sit seven to eight minutes before serving.

Recommended Wines

Torres Gran Vina Sol

Torres Gran Sangre de Toro

Ingredients

Serves 2

3 oz olive oil

1 Tbsp onion, chopped

1 tsp garlic, chopped

1 medium tomato, peeled, seeded, chopped

4 oz squid rings

1/2 cup dry white wine

8 oz rice, imported, short grain

20 oz lobster and fish stock

8 jumbo shrimp, peeled, deveined

8 clams, steamed, off the shell

2 lobster tails, off the shell, 4-5 oz each

8 mussels, steamed, off the shell

8 oz sea scallops

1 pinch saffron

6 green asparagus

1 cup green peas

1 red pimiento

salt, pepper

Paella con Hortalizas

(Vegetable Paella)

Ingredients

Serves 1
2 oz olive oil
$^1/_2$ leek, white part only, chopped
1 Tbsp onion, chopped
1 Tbsp garlic, chopped
1 small tomato, peeled, seeded, chopped
2 fresh artichoke hearts
1 red bell pepper, roasted, peeled, julienne
$^1/_2$ cup cauliflower florets
2 oz green peas
4 oz rice, imported, short grain
10 oz chicken stock
1 tsp parsley, chopped
salt, pepper

Method

In earthenware casserole, heat oil; add half of the garlic, onion, leek and tomato. Cook for two minutes. Add artichokes, red bell pepper, cauliflower and peas.

Add half of chicken stock and cook on low heat for ten minutes; season with salt and pepper. Add the rest of the garlic and parsley.

Add the rice and rest of the stock. Cook for another 20 minutes or until rice is cooked. Add more stock if necessary.

NOTE: For this recipe, you may use any fresh vegetables in season.

Recommended Wines

Torres Vina Sol

Torres Gran Vina Sol

Buñuelos de Viento

(Beignet Filled with Soft Custard)

Method

Boil liquids and butter. Mix in flour, place into a 20 quart mixer and incorporate eggs. This mixture will be piped onto parchment the size of quarters, approximate one inch high. Place parchment into oil heated to 300 degrees Fahrenheit for eight minutes, or until done.

Boil all ingredients and cool.

Soft Custard filling: (can be served as a dessert on its own)
Heat the milk with the cinnamon sticks until wisps of steam appear above the surface of milk. Remove from heat.

Beat eggs and sugar in a mixing bowl until pale yellow and slightly thickened. Beating constantly, slowly pour in the hot milk in a thin stream. Return the mixture to saucepan. Stirring constantly, cook over low heat until creamy surface froth disappears and the custard thickens enough to lightly coat the spoon.

Do not let the custard come anywhere near a boil or it will curdle. Cool custard to room temperature.

Chocolate Sauce:
Mix the ingredients together to make a thick, smooth sauce.

Ingredients

Serves 10
1 cup water
1 cup milk
$^{1}/_{2}$ cup butter
1 cup all purpose flour
10 eggs

Chocolate Sauce for plate decoration:
1 cup water
2 fl oz milk
2 fl oz dark karo syrup
1 cup semi sweet chocolate
1 oz cocoa powder

Soft Custard:
1 $^{1}/_{2}$ cups milk
1 cinnamon stick
2 eggs
$^{1}/_{4}$ cup sugar
ground cinnamon

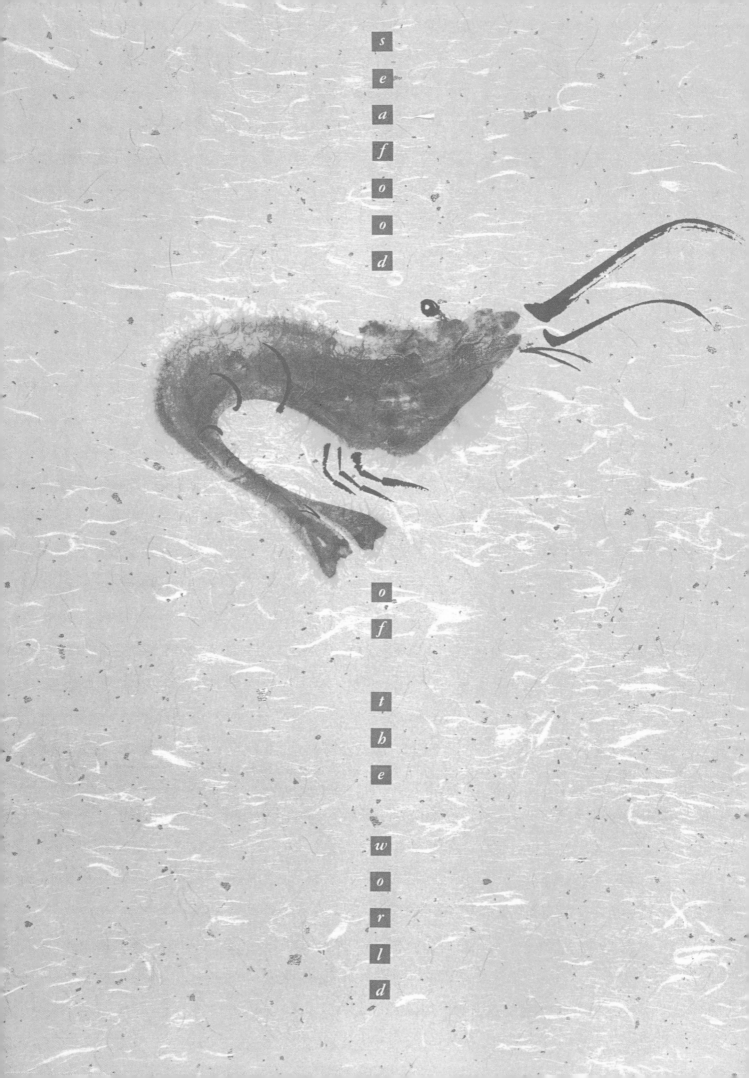

seafood of the world

3 Seafood of the World

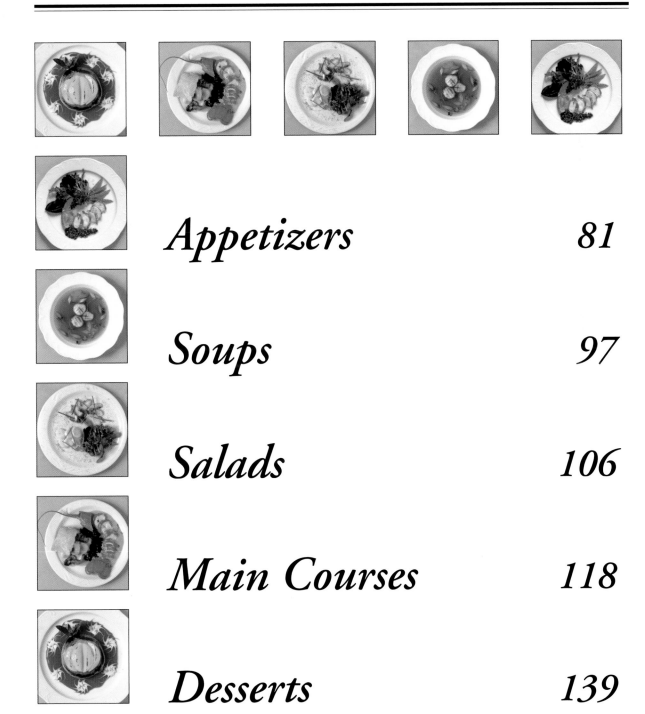

"Seafood of the World"

The "Seafood of the World" promotion was a great challenge with great rewards.

For the first time, Westin brought Master Chefs from four continents to participate in the recipe development. This was a challenge, but the recipes they developed were a great reward. The combination of the world's best ingredients with the great ability of the Master Chefs and their knowledge of different ethnic cooking methods made this promotion so unique.

Once the recipes were prepared, we paired those dishes with wines from four continents. What a way to create international friendships!

The artwork for this promotion was another first for Westin. Together with students from the University of Washington School of Art in Seattle, USA, a competition was held and the winning shrimp design was produced by Ms Yoko Sato Killian.

Menu Development Task Force

(from left to right)

Kurt H. Fischer *Vice President, Food & Beverage,* Westin Hotels & Resorts

Heinz Zasche *Pastry Chef,* The Westin Hotel, Seattle

Minao Ishizaka *Chef de Cuisine,* Caesar Park Ipanema, Rio de Janeiro

Tadashi Katoh *Chef de Cuisine,* Century Plaza Hotel, Los Angeles

Hans Günter Harms *Chef de Cuisine,* Hotel Vier Jahreszeiten, Hamburg

Lee Evans *Corporate Procurement Manager*

Marcus Dunbar *Executive Chef,* The Westin Hotel, Seattle

Fabiano Marcolini *Executive Chef,* Caesar Park Hotel, Sao Paulo

Jamie Morningstar *Chef,* Napa Valley, California

Christopher Guinn *Sous Chef,* The Westin Hotel, Seattle

Waldo Brun *Corporate Executive Chef,* Walt Disney World Swan, Orlando

Michael Quinttus *Vice President Wine Division,* Kobrand Corporation

Mark Hellbach *Executive Chef,* The Westin Resort Macau

Not Pictured: **Tylun Pang** *Executive Chef,* The Westin Kauai

"Seafood of the World"
List of Recipes

Appetizers

Soups

Salads

Main Courses

Desserts

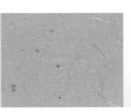

The Robert Mondavi Family

We believe the table provides one of life's great pleasures... the opportunity to slow down and savor each other's company, while enjoying great wine and food.

ROBERT MONDAVI WINERY

Braised Lobster Salad

with Ginger & Coriander Vinaigrette

Chef Mark Hellbach, The Westin Resort, Macau

Method

Remove lobster from shell, season with salt and pepper. Wrap the lobster tail with some butter into aluminium foil and braise in an oven on moderate heat for four to five minutes.

Arrange salad leaves on plate.

Mix oil, vinegar, ginger, coriander and parsley to a thick dressing.

Season with salt, pepper and a few drops of lemon juice.

Marinate the snow peas with some dressing and arrange on the plate.

Remove lobster from foil and slice into medallions, arrange on the plate and pour dressing around the lobster meat.

Ingredients

Serves 2
2 pieces Maine lobster, blanched
80 g butter
100 g Oakleaf lettuce
12 pieces Belgium endive leaves
80 g Mache lettuce
100 g snow peas, blanched
2 Tbsp chopped coriander leaves
1 Tbsp chopped parsley
15 g ginger, julienne
6 tsp vegetable oil
2 tsp sherry vinegar
salt, pepper, lemon juice

Recommended Wines

Robert Mondavi 1989 Cabernet Sauvignon

Vichon 1991 Chardonnay

Roasted Anaheim Chilli Stuffed

with Hot Pepper, Jack & Calamari

Chef Jamie Morningstar, Napa Valley, California

Ingredients

Serves 2

8 whole fresh Anaheim chillies peppers (long green) or Ortega brand canned whole Anaheim chillies

2 cups grated hot pepper Jack cheese

1 cup chopped calamari

1 pint heavy cream

1 Tbsp fresh cilantro, finely chopped

salt, freshly ground black pepper

Method

Roast peppers over a gas burner or under a broiler until the skin is charred.

Put the peppers in a brown paper bag and allow them to steam for ten minutes. Remove the skins. Split lengthwise and remove the seeds and veins.

Fill the chilli peppers with grated cheese and top the cheese with calamari. Roll the peppers to cover the cheese and calamari. Place the rolled peppers seam side down on an oiled baking sheet and bake in a 350 degrees Fahrenheit for ten minutes.

While preparing the chillies, reduce the cream by half over medium to low heat. Just before serving the chillies, add the chopped cilantro to the reduced cream, so that it will retain its bright green colour. Season with salt and pepper if needed.

Serve the chillies with a ladle of the cilantro sauce over the top of each chilli. Garnish with a whole cilantro leaf if desired.

Recommended Wines

Christian Moueix 1988 Merlot

Vichon 1991 Chevrignon

Carpaccio of Artichokes with Crayfish

and Parmesan

Chef Hans Günter Harms, Hotel Vier Jahreszeiten, Hamburg

Method

Slice artichokes bottom thinly. Season with salt, pepper, garlic and lemon juice. Sauté in olive oil.

Place them on a plate, marinate with dressing.

Make dressing of vinegar balsamico and olive oil.

Sprinkle with grated Parmesan cheese, garnish with cooked crayfish tails and cherry tomatoes.

Finish with small salad bouquet and cold tomato mousseline sauce.

Garnish with fresh herbs.

Ingredients

Serves 2
2 pieces artichokes
8 pieces crayfish, cooked
2 salad bouquet
vinegar balsamico (dressing)
olive oil
10 pieces cherry tomatoes
fresh herbs for garnish
100 g Parmesan cheese
pepper, salt
garlic
lemon juice

VICHON
1991 NAPA VALLEY
CHARDONNAY

ALCOHOL 13.5% BY VOLUME

Reommended Wine

Vichon 1991 Chardonnay

Seafood Custard

with Broccoli Sauce

Chef Minao Ishizaka, Caesar Park Ipanema, Rio de Janeiro

Ingredients

Serves 4

50 g Shiitake mushrooms, julienne
30 g Shimegi mushrooms, julienne
20 g wood mushrooms, julienne
30 g spinach purée
80 g broccoli purée
5 pieces whole eggs
4 pieces crayfish, poached
4 pieces scallops, broiled
160 ml shrimp stock
450 ml fresh cream
1 Tbsp soya sauce
4 pieces shrimp
60 g green onion, blanched, and cut into quarter inch strips
salt, pepper
3 Tbsp wine vinegar
8 pieces baby clams, poached
4 pieces oysters, poached
4 tsp tomatoes, diced, marinated with oil, sherry vinegar, chopped parsley , seasoned with salt and pepper
8 pieces broccoli tip, blanched

Method

Make the sauce with broccoli, spinach purée, cream, two egg yolks and wine vinegar and mix well. Season with salt, soya sauce and pepper.

Mix three eggs with cream and shrimp stock and season with salt and pepper.

Place the green onion strips into cocote, add the shrimp, clams, oysters and mushrooms. Pour in egg and cream mixture.

Place cocote in steamer and steam for 14 minutes. Turn cocote out and place the seafood royal on plate and arrange the broccoli.

Decorate with crayfish and place the tomato marinade on top of the royal. Pour over with the broccoli sauce.

Recommended Wines

Robert Mondavi 1990 Fumé Blanc

Vichon 1991 Chardonnay

Salmon and Turbot Carpaccio

with Lime & Olive Oil

Chef Mark Hellbach, The Westin Resort, Macau

Method

Slice the salmon fillet into a large, flat, thin slice.

Place the turbot fillet on top and roll the salmon tight around the turbot.

Wrap the salmon roll with a paper and place into the freezer for about two hours.

Cut the salmon turbot roll into very thin slices and arrange on a chilled dinner plate. Brush with olive oil and lime juice and adjust seasoning with salt and pepper.

Combine the curly endive lettuce, tomato and the cucumber strips and toss with the vinaigrette dressing.

To serve, arrange the salad in the middle of the carpaccio and garnish with strips of fresh basil.

Vinagrette Dressing:
Whisk all the ingredients together and season with salt and pepper.

Ingredients

Serves 2
180 g salmon fillet
180 g turbot fillet
80 g curly endive lettuce
40 g tomato strips
40 g cucumber strips
5 g basil strips
80 ml olive oil
20 ml lime juice
salt, pepper
50 ml *vinaigrette dressing

Vinaigrette Dressing:
150 ml white wine vinegar
200 ml sunflower seed oil
50 ml chicken stock
salt, pepper

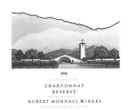

Recommended Wines

Robert Mondavi 1991 Reserve Chardonnay

Robert Mondavi 1989 Cabernet Sauvignon

Heinz Zasche

Executive Pastry Chef
The Westin Hotel, Seattle

"Baking is a joy to experience time and time again. Maybe it's the pleasure gained by watching the faces of others as they smile while taking that first bite — or maybe it's the ooh's and aah's that make all the time you spent preparing worthwhile. It's definitely the thrill of giving a gift you know the recipient will be excited about.

Where does this joy stem from? First and foremost, your work must be your love. You must truly enjoy standing on your feet in front of a hot oven day in and day out.

Getting back to the basics with simple cooking is what I strongly believe in and taste is my primary focus in preparation. If something looks wonderful but doesn't have the great taste, the diner will leave unsatisfied and your efforts have gone unnoticed.

Take the time and enjoy your efforts. Baking is a gift you give freely and reap the rewards."

- culinary philosophy of Chef Heinz Zache

The Westin Hotel, Seattle,
Washington, USA

Stuffed Zucchini Flower

with Mushroom & Santa Barbara Bay Shrimp Mousse

Chef Tadashi Katoh, Chef de Cuisine, Century Plaza Hotel, Los Angeles

Method

Chop four pieces of shrimp tail and press through a fine sieve, allow to cool in a bowl of ice, season with salt and pepper, add one egg yolk and mix well. Add half cup of cream little by little.

Add the chopped mushroom and mix. Stuff into zucchini flower and keep cool.

Sauté shrimp heads, add chopped vegetables and sauté well. Flame with the cognac and then add the tomato paste, white wine, fish stock and reduce almost completely.

Add the cream and bring to a boil. Simmer for ten minutes. Strain the stock through a sieve, thicken the sauce with butter, seasoning with salt and pepper.

Steam the stuffed zucchini flower in steamer for six minutes.

Sauté the shrimp tails in butter and season.

Sweat the diced tomato in butter and season.

Arrange zucchini flowers, shrimp tails and diced tomato on a plate. Add the chopped basil into sauce and pour on middle of the plate.

Decorate with basil tip.

Recommended Wines

Vichon 1991 Chardonnay

Robert Mondavi 1990 Fumé Blanc

Ingredients

Serves 2

4 pieces zucchini flowers, clean
12 pieces Santa Barbara Bay shrimp, with head on
1 egg yolk
2 oz mushrooms, chopped (sauté in butter and let cool)
2 tsp shallots, chopped, seasoned
1 oz carrots, chopped
1 oz onions, chopped
1 oz celery, chopped
1 oz leeks, chopped
1/2 oz garlic, chopped
1 oz olive oil
2 Tbsp tomato paste
1 cup white wine
1 cup fish stock
2 1/2 cups cream
4 bunches basil, fresh (keep the tip for decoration)
1 fresh tomato, diced
5 oz butter
1 oz cognac
salt, pepper

Steamed Mussels

with Black Bean & Chilli Sauce

Chef Tylun Pang, The Westin Kauai, Hawaii

Ingredients

Serves 1
5 whole green lipped mussels
2 Tbsp Oriental fermented black beans (soaked, rinsed and mashed)
1 piece leek
$^1/_2$ red pepper
$^1/_2$ yellow pepper
$^1/_2$ tsp garlic, chopped
$^1/_2$ tsp ginger, chopped
1 tsp chilli paste
1 Tbsp oyster sauce
$^1/_2$ cup white wine
2 Tbsp butter

Method

Steam mussels with quarter cup of white wine and one tablespoon butter. Remove top shell and prepare sauce.

Sauce:
Sauté black beans with remaining butter. Add ginger, garlic, white wine, oyster sauce and chilli paste.
Serve sauce over steamed mussels.
Stir fry leeks with yellow and red peppers.
Garnish as shown in picture.

Recommended Wines

Christian Moueix 1988 Merlot

Cape Mentelle 1989 Shiraz

Aumoniere of Mushrooms

with Tofu Mousse

Chef Minao Ishizaka, Caesar Park Ipanema, Rio de Janeiro

Method

Marinate the shrimps, scallops with olive oil, salt, peppercorns, red wine and mirin.

Mix the wasabi, egg yolks, cream, salt, sugar, grape seed oil and sherry wine vinegar as you would in making mayonnaise.

Make crepes as you would normally.

Arrange the aumoniere and marinated scallops and pour the wasabi sauce.

Place the tofu mousse, marinated shrimp and mushrooms in the middle of the crepe and tie with blanched chives.

Decorate with Oba leaf and tomato.

Ingredients

Serves 2
10 g Shimeji mushrooms
8 g Shiitake mushrooms
60 g tofu, mashed, mixed with cream, soya sauce with salt and pepper

Marinade:
4 shrimp, poached
12 scallops
80 ml olive oil
1 1/2 tsp salt, black peppercorns
15 g pink peppercorns
30 ml red wine
mirin

Wasabi sauce:
1 pinch lemon skin, finely chopped
15 g Wasabi
3 egg yolks
1 Tbsp cream
1 Tbsp sugar
1 1/2 Tbsp grape seed oil
1 1/2 Tbsp sherry wine vinegar

Recommended Wines

Deinhard 1990 Riesling Dry

Robert Mondavi 1991 Reserve Chardonnay

Parfait of Fennel
with Grilled Seafood Sauce Rouille

Chef Hans Günter Harms, Hotel Vier Jahreszeiten, Hamburg

Ingredients

Serves 2
Fennel Parfait:
300 g fennel purée
150 g butter
4 pieces egg yolks
125 ml whipped cream
5 pieces gelée leaves

Sauce Rouille:
1 red pepper, diamond cut
1 onion, chopped
2 cloves garlic, chopped
$^{1}/_{2}$ tsp sambal olek
3 egg yolks
5 Tbsp olive oil
salt, pepper
lemon juice
100 ml white wine

Seafood:
10 pieces langoustines, grilled
200 g turbot fillet, grilled
200 g salmon fillet, grilled
200 g sole fillet, grilled
10 scallops, grilled

Method

Fennel Parfait:
Clarify butter and prepare light sauce hollandaise with egg yolks. Layer gelée, fennel purée and whipped cream under hollandaise sauce in a terrine and set to chill.

Sauce Rouille:
Fry onion, garlic and red pepper. Season with salt, pepper, lemon juice and sambal olek. Deglaze with white wine; if it is cold, mix it in a blender.

Presentation:
When firm, turn fennel parfait out of terrine bowl onto plate. Dress with sauce rouille and surround with grilled seafood. Garnish with fresh herbs.

Recommended Wines

Deinhard 1990 Riesling Dry

Vichon 1991 Chevrignon

Almond Mussels

Chef Fabiano Marcolini, Caesar Park Hotel, Sao Paulo

Method

Crush the garlic and parsley, then add the soft butter. Soak the brioche in wine for a minute until it is a bit soft.

Take excess wine off and add to butter, garlic and parsley. Mix wet brioche with the almonds, season with pepper, salt. Make smooth all ingredients.

Preheat the oven at 200 degrees Celsius, wash and clean mussels under water. After putting them in a hot pan, cover and shake for a few minutes until opened.

Leave to cool a bit, put the almond mixture on top of each open mussel and cook in the oven five to six minutes.

Mussels have to be eaten very hot. We suggest eating them with one glass full of ice; add one dose Armagnac and one slice of orange. Top it up with dry white wine, very cold, mix and drink at once.

Ingredients

Serves 2
2 kg fresh mussels in their shells
1 clove garlic
2 pieces parsley, chopped
500 g butter, softened
30 g brioche
2 or 3 Tbsp of white wine
100 g salt, ground black pepper

Recommended Wine
Deinhard 1990 Riesling Dry

Marcus Dunbar

Executive Chef
The Westin Hotel, Seattle

The Westin Hotel, Seattle,
Washington, USA

"Cooking is an offering, and it is a gesture of care and love to bring one's own creation to life, however humble or simple. Sharing food is rich in symbolism of our deepest human needs. A meal's aim is to stimulate both the eye and the appetite.

My philosophy towards food and cooking stems directly from my childhood. Simply put, I feel you should cook and eat what you enjoy and have fun while you're doing it. That's really all you need to know to begin to make your own food memories."

- culinary philosophy of Chef Marcus Dunbar

More than half of Chef Dunbar's nearly 20 years of culinary and managerial experience was gained overseas.

For the past seven years, Dunbar has successfully managed kitchens at Seattle's Westin.

The 35-year-old Redmond resident plays soccer and coaches a youth team for the Washington Soccer Association.

Although much of his time is now spent in management and directing the four Sous Chefs who work for him, his passion has not changed.

Yellow Tail, White Rice & Brunoise Vegetables

with Wasabi Cream Sauce

Chef Waldo Brun, Corporate Executive Chef, Walt Disney World Swan, Florida

Method

Combine sushi rice with rice wine vinegar and vegetables brunoise.

Form rice into oval shaped ball and surround with two slices Yellow Tail.

Mix wasabi paste, mayonnaise and rice wine vinegar. Cut vegetable garnishes as shown.

Place sauce on plate and arrange ingredients as shown in picture.

Ingredients

Serves 2
1 cup Sushi rice, cooked
1 Tbsp rice wine vinegar
1 oz zucchini brunoise
1 oz yellow squash brunoise
1 oz cucumber brunoise
4 sliced Yellow Tail fillet

Sauce:
2 tsp Wasabi, mixed with water to form paste
4 oz mayonnaise
1 Tbsp rice wine vinegar

Garnish:
cucumber, cut into thin strips
carrot, cut into thin strips
tomato

Recommended Wines

Vichon 1991 Chardonnay

Robert Mondavi 1991 Sauvignon Blanc

Sea Urchin and Salmon Tartar

on Wild Rice Blini

Chef Mark Hellbach, The Westin Resort, Macau

Ingredients

Serves 2
240 g salmon fillet, finely cubed
100 g sea urchin roe
60 g shallots, finely chopped
40 g cucumber, finely chopped
5 g dill, chopped
$\frac{1}{2}$ tsp wasabi mustard
1 juice of lemon
salt, pepper
2 Tbsp olive oil
cayenne pepper
100 g wild rice, boiled
100 g pancake batter
180 g curly Frisee lettuce
fresh dill leaves

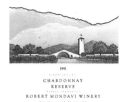

Method

Take sea urchin roe, separate four whole nice pieces and keep for decoration. Chop the rest into small pieces.

Mix the olive oil, shallots, cucumber, chopped dill and wasabi mustard to a smooth paste.

Add the salmon and chopped sea urchin, mix very well and season to taste with salt, pepper, lemon juice and a pinch of Cayenne pepper. Marinate this tartar for about 15 minutes.

Mix wild rice and pancake. Batter and bake four equal sized blinis about five to six centimetres in diameter.

Place blinis in center of plates. Scoop two tablespoons of salmon tartar on top and decorate with the remaining sea urchin roe.

Sprinkle the Curly Frisee lettuce leaves around and decorate with dill leaves.

Recommended Wines

Robert Mondavi 1991 Reserve Chardonnay

Vichon 1991 Chardonnay

Seafood Ravioli

Chef Fabiano Marcolini, Caesar Park Hotel, Sao Paulo

Method

Prepare the noodles and pass through cylinder. Cut and sauté all the seafood.

Cut the noodles with ravioli mold and fill the white noodles with lobster, the green noodles with scallops and the red noodles with prawns.

Seal edges of each ravioli by brushing with egg yolk, pressing together gently. Cook in hot boiling water until al denté.

Serve with three sauces: tomato, cheese and broccoli. Put the sauces divided in three parts on the plate and put six ravioli in each plate in a round circle.

Ingredients

Serves 3
120 g beetroot noodle paste
120 g spinach noodle paste
120 g fresh scallops
80 g prawns
salt, pepper to taste

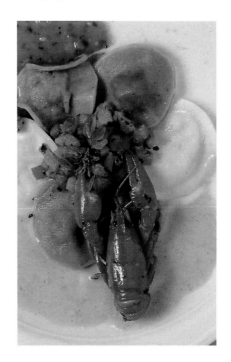

VICHON
1991 NAPA VALLEY
CHARDONNAY

ALCOHOL 12.5% BY VOLUME

Recommended Wines

Vichon 1991 Chardonnay

Vichon 1991 Chevrignon

Salmon & Egg Yolk Sushi

with Lobster & Asparagus in Sesame Sauce

Chef Minao Ishizaka, Caesar Park Ipanema, Rio de Janeiro

Ingredients

Serves 2
Salmon & Egg Yolk Sushi:
70 g smoked salmon, sliced
6 g egg yolk
28 ml rice vinegar
2 Tbsp sugar
1 pinch cornstarch

Sesame Seed Sauce:
70 g sesame paste
20 ml white wine vinegar
60 g sugar
1 piece egg yolk
3 Tbsp olive oil
1 Tbsp soya sauce
15 ml cream
20 g soy bean paste
1 Tbsp white sesame seeds, roasted

Garnish:
2 pieces lobster, poached
12 pieces green asparagus tips

Method

Mix all ingredients for salmon and egg yolk sushi, except smoked salmon.

Place the bowl with seasoned ingredients in hot water and mix with wooden spatula until thick. Let cool.

Make small ball shape and wrap with smoked salmon.

Mix all ingredients for sesame seed sauce together in a blender.

Slice lobster tail and arrange on plate with salmon and egg yolk sushi.

Pour the sauce and decorate with lobster claw and green asparagus.

Recommended Wines

Deinhard 1990 Riesling Dry

Robert Mondavi 1991 Fumé Blanc

Scallops Soup

Chef Minao Ishizaka, Caesar Park Ipanema, Rio de Janeiro

Method

Soak the dried Shiitake mushrooms and julienne.

Put some oil in a pan, sauté the diced onion, turnip shoots, carrots and asparagus.

Add fish "fumé" and white wine.

Add a little Aji-no-moto and soya sauce for taste.

Sear scallops on the broiler.

Add to the liquid in the pan and bring to simmer.

Garnish and serve.

Ingredients

Serves 2
8 scallops
10 dried Shiitake mushrooms
100 g turnip shoots
1 carrot, cut into floral shape
1 onion, diced
4 asparagus
1 dl cognac
1 l fish "fumé"
soya sauce
Aji-no-moto (Japanese seasoning)
1 dl white wine

Recommended Wine

Deinhard 1990 Riesling Dry

Minao Ishizaka

Executive Chef of Mariko Restaurant
Caesar Park Ipanema, Rio de Janeiro

Born in the city of Shizuoka, Japan, Chef Minao Ishizaka began his professional career in 1972, in Tokyo. In 1982 he decided to go to Brazil where he worked the following four years.

His culinary skills produced an invitation from Japan Airlines where he was luckily "stolen" by the Caesar Park Ipanema Hotel in 1989, and made the hotel's Mariko Restaurant the most awarded Japanese cuisine in town.

His preferred hobby is fishing, very appropriate for someone who deals so much with fish in his daily routine! Among his culinary skills are ice-carving, vegetable decoration, Japanese classical Kaiseki, seasonal and international dishes.

Caesar Park Ipanema,
Rio de Janeiro, Brazil

Florida Fish Stew

Chef Waldo Brun, Corporate Executive Chef, Walt Disney Swan, Florida

Method

In soup pot, heat olive oil and sauté garlic. Add onions, fennel, leeks and carrots. Continue to sauté, adding saffron and cracked black pepper.

Deglaze with white wine and Pernod. Add chicken stock. Add seafood and poach until done.

Add green and yellow squash and chopped fennel tops.

Season the soup as needed and serve as shown.

Ingredients

Serves 2
2 oz olive oil
1 oz garlic, chopped
3 oz onions, diced
3 oz leeks, julienne
3 oz carrots, julienne
pinch saffron
1/2 oz cracked black pepper
4 oz white wine
2 oz Pernod
4 pt chicken stock
3 oz yellow squash, julienne
3 oz green zucchini, julienne
pinch fennel tops, chopped
3 oz fish, cut in 1/2 inch cubes
4 small shrimp
4 mussels
2 clams

Recommended Wines

Vichon 1991 Chardonnay

Robert Mondavi 1991 Reserve Chardonnay

Pacific Seafood Stew

with Japanese Pumpkin & Nori

Chef Tylun Pang, The Westin Kauai, Hawaii

Ingredients

Serves 1

1 calamari with tentacles, cleaned
2 mussels
3 Manila clams
2 sea urchin roe
1 oz red snapper
2 oz white wine
2 oz heavy cream
$^1/_2$ tsp shallots, chopped
1 Tbsp butter
Japanese pumpkin, julienne
Nori - dried seaweed
2 oz fish stock

Method

Clean and prepare all seafood ahead of time. Sauté seafood, except sea urchin roe, with butter and shallots for one minute.

Deglaze pan with white wine and fish stock. Cook until seafood is done.

Remove cooked seafood to serving plate. Add heavy cream to remaining liquid and simmer until slightly thickened. Finish sauce with sea urchin roe and pour over the other cooked seafood.

Garnish with the Japanese pumpkin julienne and Nori strips and serve.

Recommended Wines

Dienhard 1990 Riesling Dry

Robert Mondavi 1991 Reserve Chardonnay

Double Boiled Crayfish Essence

with Crab Meat Wonton & Kam Wah Ham

Chef Mark Hellbach, The Westin Resort, Macau

Method

Mix crab meat, red chillies, minced pork, coriander leaves and sesame oil, season with salt and pepper.

Fill a teaspoon of crab meat mix into wonton wrappers and fold into small triangles, sealing edges with salted water and pressing together.

Poach in the consommé for 30-40 seconds.

Serve with the crayfish consommé and sprinkle some Yunnan ham julienne on top.

Ingredients

Serves 2
16 pieces wonton skin (6 cm square)
100 g crab meat
5 g red chillies
5 g chopped coriander leaves
20 g minced pork
4 drops sesame oil
1 l crayfish consommé
20 g Yunnan ham, julienne fine

Recommended Wines

Vichon 1991 Chevrignon

Vichon 1991 Chardonnay

Oyster Chowder

with Almond Cornbread

Chef Jamie Morningstar, Napa Valley, California

Ingredients

Serves 2
4 oz bacon, diced
1 cup onions, diced
1 ¹/₂ cup mushrooms, sliced
1 ¹/₂ cup medium dry sherry
4 cloves garlic, minced
2 ¹/₂ cups clam juice
3 cups milk
1 Tbsp cornstarch (optional, for thickening)
1 cup scallions
1 juice of lemon
cayenne
salt to taste
1 cup oysters
cornbread, sliced

Method

Sauté the chopped bacon over medium heat in a saucepan large enough to hold the entire soup.

When the bacon is browned, remove the excess grease and add the onions, mushrooms, sherry and garlic. Simmer together until sherry is almost gone.

Add the clam juice and bring to a simmer. Let mixture reduce by half.

Then add the milk and bring to a simmer. Let the soup simmer together about ten minutes.

You can hold this over a hot water bath until ready for serving.

About three minutes before serving, add the oysters, scallions and lemon juice.

Season with cayenne and salt, serve over a slice of cornbread in a large soup bowl.

Garnish the top with a few chopped scallions if desired.

Recommended Wines

Deinhard 1990 Riesling Dry

Vichon 1991 Chevrignon

Goujonnent of Sole
Leeks and Shiitake Soup

Chef Tadashi Katoh, Chef de Cuisine, Century Plaza Hotel, Los Angeles

Method

Place the fish stock in pan and bring to a boil.

Add the leeks and simmer until cooked. Add the Shiitake mushrooms, sole and poach until cooked. Add the potatoes.

Remove the sole, potatoes, Shiitake mushrooms and leeks and place in soup bowl.

Add the butter and beat with whisk. Add the chopped chives, season with salt and pepper.

Pour the soup over the garnish and sprinkle with chervil on top.

Ingredients

Serves 2

2 pieces whole Dover sole, cleaned, filleted and cut into strips

6 oz leeks, diced into $^1/_2$ inch cubes

4 pieces Shiitake mushrooms, sliced

12 pieces small turned potatoes, cooked

40 fl oz fish stock

2 Tbsp chives, chopped

2 oz butter

4 bunch chervil

salt, pepper

Recommended Wines

Vichon 1991 Chardonnay

Robert Mondavi 1991 Fumé Blanc

Hamburger Tassen-Bouillon

with Oysters

Chef Hans Günter Harms, Hotel Vier Jahreszeiten, Hamburg

Method

Lightly poach the oysters in the consommé. Remove oysters and set aside. Reduce the oyster juice and cream double in two separate pans.

Dice cut the small Haricot verts and blanch them. Mix the Haricots, poached oysters and reduced double cream to form an oyster ragout. Heat until very warm.

Serve the oyster consommé in a demi-tasse cup. Put the cup on a large plate. On the plate, also place one puff pastry cup.

Fill the puff pastry with the oysters ragout.

Garnish the plate with small salad of beet as shown in picture.

Repeat for each plate.

Ingredients

Serves 2
30 pieces oysters
8 dl oyster consommé
10 pieces small puff pastry cups (also known as puff pastry bouchées)
2 dl cream double (48% milk fat)
200 g Haricot verts
200 g beet, julienne

Recommended Wines

Deinhard 1990 Riesling Dry

Vichon 1989 Chevrignon

Octopus and Scallop Salad

with Spicy Mustard Vinaigrette

Chef Tylun Pang, The Westin Kauai, Hawaii

Ingredients

Serves 2

2 oz octopus, cooked and sliced

3 pieces large scallops, cooked and sliced in half round

1 cup mixed salad greens, seasonal

2 Tbsp *mustard vinaigrette

4 sprigs fresh chives

cayenne pepper

**Mustard Vinaigrette*

1/2 cup salad oil

1/4 cup cider vinegar

1 egg yolk

2 Tbsp mustard

1 oz hot water

1/2 oz lemon juice

Tabasco sauce

salt, to taste

Method

Mustard Vinaigrette:

Whip all ingredients together, except salad oil. Slowly add salad oil until dressing is of a creamy texture, adjust seasoning.

Arrange salad leaves, sliced octopus and scallops on platter.

Dress seafood lightly with mustard dressing. Sprinkle cayenne pepper over salad and garnish with fresh chives.

Recommended Wines

Deinhard 1990 Riesling Dry

Vichon 1991 Chevrignon

Spicy Swordfish
with Crispy Wonton

Chef Mark Hellbach, The Westin Resort, Macau

Method

Dressing:

Whisk in the ingredients for the dressing until well blended. Season with salt and pepper.

Place deep fried wonton between two spatulas to keep them flat.

Sauté mushrooms, cut into halves, in olive oil.

Toss salad with dressing. Toss in strips of pepper. Arrange all on a plate.

Pan fry slices of swordfish and keep warm.

Tip the salad with the fish, a piece of wonton and bell pepper.

Garnish with flowers.

Recommended Wines

Vichon 1991 Chardonnay

Vichon 1991 Chevrignon

Ingredients

Serves 2

150 g swordfish, cleaned
50 g baby spinach, cleaned
30 g Radiccio leaves
30 g yellow, red, green pepper strips
20 g Shiitake mushrooms
10 g straw mushrooms
5 g roasted almonds, sliced
2 pieces deep fried wonton skin
flowers for decoration

Dressing:

2 ¹/₂ dl red wine vinegar
1 dl sesame oil
4 dl corn oil
1 Tbsp Chinese chilli sauce
50 g chopped coriander leaves
50 g chopped spring onions
20 g chopped ginger
2 cloves garlic, chopped
salt, pepper

Warm Potato Salad in Green Sauce

with Smoked Halibut

Chef Hans Günter Harms, Hotel Vier Jahreszeiten, Hamburg

Ingredients

Serves 2
10 pieces large potatoes
2 pieces shallots, sliced thinly
2 dl seafood or fish consommé
4 tsp of mixed fresh herbs
2 dl sauce vert
6 dl champagne vinegar
1 kg halibut fillet

Marinade:
80 g salt
1 ¹/₂ l water
1 tsp Herbs de Provence
4 cloves garlic
1 tsp paprika

Method

Simmer for ten minutes the ingredients for marinade. After it is cold, marinate the halibut for 12 hours. Smoke the halibut for ten minutes at 180 degrees Celsius.

Potato Salad:

Cook the potatoes in light vinegar water, cut in round slices, marinate with shallots, vinegar and consommé.

Serve the potato salad on a plate, heat lightly in a microwave, cover with sauce vert, garnish with smoked halibut and small salad bouquet of the season.

Recommended Wines
Robert Mondavi 1990 Fumé Blanc
Robert Mondavi 1991 Sauvignon Blanc

Salade Orientale au Thon

Chef Minao Ishizaka, Caesar Park Ipanema, Rio de Janeiro

Method

Marinate tuna for two hours with marinade ingredients.

Slice and sear tuna in hot pan.

Slice thinly the avocado, cucumber and mango.

Arrange on plate with other ingredients.

Mix ingredients for dressing together and dress the salad.

Garnish and serve.

Ingredients

Serves 2
4 tsp gergelim
1 Red lettuce, small
1 Red cabbage, small
2 tomatoes, sliced
100 g corn
16 asparagus
250 g tuna fish
1 mango
1 avocado
1 cucumber
Dressing:
a pinch of wasabi
20 ml rice vinegar
50 ml olive oil
1 tsp soy sauce
Marinade:
3 Tbsp vinegar
3 Tbsp sugar
a pinch Aji-no-moto
3 tsp paste of soya
200 g mirin (Japanese sweet sake)

Recommended Wines

Robert Mondavi 1991 Reserve Chardonnay

Christian Moueix 1988 Merlot

Tadashi Katoh

Chef de Cuisine
Century Plaza Hotel & Tower,
Los Angeles

Born and raised in Fukushima, Japan, Chef Katoh has served in some of the premier hotels of both Japan and Canada.

Although his style reflects his Japanese heritage, Chef Katoh's forte is classic French cuisine, with an accent on "cuisine naturelle."

In 1979, he was honored as National Winner and Grand Champion of the First Wiser Deluxe Culinary Classic — the country's highest distinction for a Chef. During his illustrious career, he has also been bestowed with four gold medals at the Grand Salon Culinary Championships in Montreal, four silver medals at the Taste of Toronto Culinary Competition, and a bronze medal in the Simokitazawa Ice Carving Competition in Tokyo.

Century Plaza Hotel & Tower,
Los Angeles, California, USA

110

Cured Salmon and Grouper Roulade

with Mache Lettuce

Chef Waldo Brun, Corporate Executive Chef, Walt Disney World Swan, Florida

Method

Thinly slice the salmon horizontally into two or three thin, flat slices. Place fresh grouper strips in center and roll tightly.

Cure salmon rolls in sugar, salt and freshly chopped dill mixture for 48 hours.

Cook and peel quail eggs and cut in half.

Remove salmon rolls from mix and slice.

Prepare sauce, mixing ingredients as you would with dressing.

Arrange salad on plate as shown in picture, place the sliced salmon rolls and serve.

Note: This salad is to be prepared 48 hours in advance.

Ingredients

Serves 1
1 side fresh salmon
1 lb fresh grouper
2 quail eggs, hard boiled
2 oz Mache lettuce
1 tomato, peeled and seeded
1 lb sugar
1/2 lb salt
2 oz fresh dill
Sauce:
2 oz mayonnaise
1/2 Tbsp fresh dill, chopped
1 oz parsley juice
salt, pepper to taste
1/2 oz honey

Recommended Wines

Deinhard 1990 Riesling Dry

Robert Mondavi 1990 Fumé Blanc

Warm Salad of Abalone

Mussels & Tiger Prawns

Chef Tylun Pang, The Westin Kauai, Hawaii

Ingredients

Serves 1
1 oz abalone, cooked and sliced
2 pieces green lipped mussels
2 pieces Manila tiger prawns, peeled and deveined
$^1/_2$ tsp shallots
1 Tbsp butter
2 oz white wine

Dressing:
$^1/_2$ cup olive oil
1 tsp lemon juice
$^1/_2$ tsp sherry vinegar
1 cup mixed salad greens (Frisee, Red Oak, Green Leaf)

Method

Melt butter, add shallots, shellfish, seafood and white wine and simmer lightly until cooked. Remove and toss with dressing.

Whisk ingredients for dressing together until well blended.

Serve salad in abalone shell or salad plate.

Garnish with strips of fresh dill.

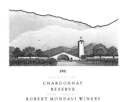

Recommended Wines
Robert Mondavi 1991 Reserve Chardonnay
Robert Mondavi 1989 Cabernet Sauvignon

Sauteed Cristal Prawns

and Sesame Salad

Chef Mark Hellbach, The Westin Resort, Macau

Method

Clean, devein and wash prawns well.

Sauté prawns with garlic and chillies, season with salt and pepper.

Deglaze with the water-diluted cornstarch.

Mix ingredients for vinaigrette well.

Arrange on the salad leaves coated with sesame oil vinaigrette.

Sprinkle with black and white sesame seeds.

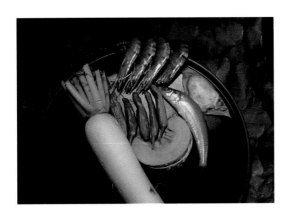

Ingredients

Serves 4
28 pieces medium prawns
5 g chopped garlic
10 g chopped red chillies
1/2 tsp cornstarch
10 Tbsp water
1 tsp white and black sesame
100 g Butter lettuce leaves
60 g Red Chiccore
100 g curly endive

Vinaigrette:
6 Tbsp white vinegar
salt, pepper
4 drops sesame oil
18 Tbsp vegetable oil

Recommended Wines

Vichon 1991 Chardonnay

Vichon 1991 Chevrignon

Warm Crab Caesar Salad

Chef Jamie Morningstar, Napa Valley, California

Ingredients

Serves 2
2 cup eggplant
2 heads garlic
$^1/_2$ cup pure olive oil
4 oz crab meat
$^1/_4$ oz lemon juice
$^1/_2$ tsp dill, dried
salt, cracked black pepper to taste
4 cup Romaine lettuce
2 cup croutons, optional

Note: Use pure olive oil when cooking to avoid bitter after-taste.

Method

Prepare the eggplant by cutting into strips two inches long and half inch wide. Salt these strips and set aside to drain excess liquid while garlic is roasting.

Cut off the tops of the garlic, so that all the cloves are exposed, and brush with olive oil. Season with cracked black pepper and wrap in foil.

Bake for one hour at 400 degrees Fahrenheit.

These first two steps can be done ahead of time and just set aside until needed.

Heat the oil until smoking in a medium size sauté pan. Add eggplant and sauté until golden brown. Add roasted garlic, crab, lemon juice and dill. Sauté together for 30 seconds and season with salt and pepper.

In a large salad bowl, toss together the Romaine lettuce and sauteed ingredients quickly.

Serve immediately and garnish with croutons if desired.

Recommended Wines

Robert Mondavi 1989 Cabernet Sauvignon

Robert Mondavi 1991 Fumé Blanc

Salad of White & Green Asparagus

with Grilled Sturgeon

Chef Hans Günter Harms, Hotel Vier Jahreszeiten, Hamburg

Method

Peel both types of asparagus, blanch them and marinate with a little champagne vinegar, asparagus consommé and grape kernel oil.

Keep asparagus tips for garnish.

Mix the rest of the champagne vinegar, asparagus consommé and grape kernel oil, season with salt and pepper and marinate the asparagus.

Garnish with salad bouquet.

Slice sturgeon fillet, grill and dress on plate.

Arrange and finish with sauce rouille.

Ingredients

Serves 4

500 g green asparagus
500 g white asparagus
4 large tomatoes for concasse
1 dl champagne vinegar
1 dl asparagus consommé
2 dl grape kernel oil
2 dl sauce rouille
1 kg sturgeon fillet
10 pieces small salad bouquet of the season

Recommended Wines

Deinhard 1990 Riesling Dry

Robert Mondavi 1991 Fumé Blanc

Mark Hellbach
Director of Kitchens, Food & Beverage
The Westin Resort, Macau

Mark Hellbach was born 1951 in Switzerland where he grew up, studied and completed his culinary training in 1969.

Spending a few years in hotels in Switzerland, perfecting his skills and gaining experience, he moved to London in 1973. It was there that he was introduced to some Asian customs and culture and his interest in Oriental food grew. After a brief stay, he joined Westin Hotels & Resorts at the Philippine Plaza Hotel in Manila, Phillipines. He was promoted to Director of Kitchens, Food & Beverage at the Westin Resort, Macau, which opened early 1993.

The Westin Resort, Coloane Ilha, Macau

116

Salade de Saumon et Crevettes

Chef Minao Ishizaka, Caesar Park Ipanema, Rio de Janeiro

Method

Mix ingredients for marinade in a large bowl.

Marinate the cooked seafood, tomatoes and soya shoots with the marinade mix.

Soak the Kikurage for a little while, slice.

Blanch soya sheets, turnip shoots, Kikurage and carrots.

Dressing:

Whisk dressing together and dress the salad greens.

Slice seafood into bite size pieces and arrange on plate.

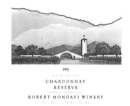

Recommended Wines

Robert Mondavi 1991 Reserve Chardonnay

Robert Mondavi 1991 Sauvignon Blanc

Ingredients

Serves 4

500 g fresh salmon, cooked
150 g octopus, cooked
150 g squid, cooked
1 Endive lettuce
150 g Kikurage (Japanese mushrooms)
16 turnip shoots, sliced
1 carrot, sliced
3 tomatoes, concasse
parsley, chopped
4 shrimp, cooked
150 g soya shoots

Marinade:

200 g paste of soya
100 g garlic
rice vinegar
sugar
2 egg yolks
2 tsp handashi (Japanese fish spice)
2 Tbsp mirin

Dressing:

2 dl white wine
soya sauce
1 lime
1 tsp handashi
salt, pepper

Lobster with Scallops & Shrimp

in Puff Pastry

Chef Waldo Brun, Corporate Executive Chef, Walt Disney World Swan, Florida

Ingredients

Serves 1
3 scallops
2 shrimp
1 ¹/₂ oz shallots, finely chopped
1 ¹/₂ garlic, finely chopped
2 medium morels
2 oz white wine
8 oz cream
1 lb Maine lobster
3 oz spinach, julienne
4 Tbsp clarified butter
2 oz lobster butter
4 oz cream
¹/₂ oz brandy
salt, pepper to taste
1 sheet puff pastry
2 oz eggwash

Method

Sauté half of the shallots and garlic in clarified butter, add shrimp, scallops and the morels.

Deglaze with white wine, reduce then add cream. Reduce to desired consistency and season with salt and pepper.

Steam or boil lobster for approximately seven minutes. Remove tail meat and slice as shown.

Reserve part of the shell (tail and head) to decorate the plate.

Sauté spinach in whole butter and shallots, season.

Lobster Sauce:

Sauté shallots, deglaze with brandy, add cream and finish with lobster butter.

Cut puff pastry into a square, eggwash and bake.

Arrange as shown.

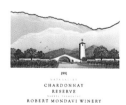

Recommended Wines

Robert Mondavi 1991 Reserve Chardonnay

Deinhard 1990 Riesling Dry

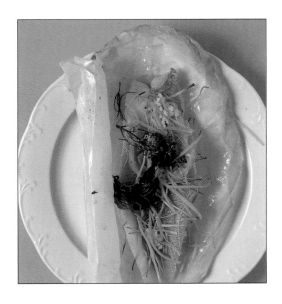

Baked Onaga

with Pancetta & Herbs

Chef Tylun Pang, The Westin Kauai, Hawaii

Method

Clean and remove scales from the snapper.

Cut parchment paper large enough to wrap fish. Place fish on oiled paper, season with salt and pepper.

Place sliced pancetta and vegetable julienne on fish. Drizzle wine and olive oil over fish, place herb sprigs on fish and close parchment paper by folding ends. Bake at 400 degrees Fahrenheit until done.

Serve snapper in paper.

Ingredients

Serves 4
1 whole red snapper, 10 oz or 8 oz fillet (skin on)
1/2 oz pancetta, sliced
1/4 oz leeks, julienne
1/4 oz carrots, julienne
1 sprig fresh thyme
1 sprig fresh oregano
1 Tbsp olive oil
2 Tbsp white wine
salt, pepper to taste
1 piece parchment paper

Recommended Wines

Cape Mentelle 1989 Shiraz

Christian Moueix 1988 Merlot

Salmon Grille Sauce au Safran

Chef Minao Ishizaka, Caesar Park Ipanema, Rio de Janeiro

Ingredients

Serves 4
1 kg salmon
2 dl olive oil
100 g tomato concentrate
50 g "dende" oil
2 tsp garlic, chopped
1 tsp grated gergelim
2 dl fish "fumé"
1 dl white wine
1 dl coconut milk
soya sauce

Garnish:
2 mangoes
1/2 tsp saffron

Method

Cut four fillets of the salmon and grill in some olive oil.

Heat the rest of the olive oil and place the chopped garlic, gergelim, concentrate of tomatoes and "dende" oil.

Reduce the sauce and add the white wine, saffron, fish fumé, coconut milk and soya sauce.

Garnish with mangoes and serve with sauce.

Recommended Wines

Vichon 1991 Chardonnay

Robert Mondavi 1991 Sauvignon Blanc

Glazed Sea Bass with Black Sesame Seeds

and Green Onion Pancakes

Chef Tylun Pang, The Westin Kauai, Hawaii

Method

Black Sesame Seeds and Green Onion Pancakes:
Mix flour, egg and milk until all lumps are gone. Fold in black sesame seeds and chopped green onions.

Let rest for half an hour before cooking. Prepare little crepes on an oiled crepe pan.

Basting Sauce:
Mix well until sugar is dissolved. Use to baste sea bass while cooking.

Sea Bass:
Heat peanut oil, sear sea bass on both sides. Discard oil, return to stove, cook on moderate heat, basting constantly with sauce until fish is evenly glazed.

Serve fish with crepes and garnish with lettuce leaf, cooked asparagus spears, carrots and Daikon julienne.

Recommended Wines
Christian Moueix 1988 Merlot

Vichon 1991 Chardonnay

Ingredients

Serves 1
3 oz sea bass fillet, skin on
1 Tbsp peanut oil

Basting Sauce:
1/2 cup soya sauce
1/4 cup sake
1/2 cup mirin
1/2 cup sugar

Black Sesame Seeds and Green Onion Pancakes:
1/2 cup flour
1/2 cup milk
1 whole egg
2 Tbsp green onions, chopped fine
2 tsp black sesame seeds

Garnish:
2 lettuce leaves
3 asparagus spears, blanched
1/2 carrots, julienne finely
1/2 Daikon, julienne finely

Assorted Seafood Lasagne

with Vermouth Sauce

Chef Mark Hellbach, The Westin Resort, Macau

Method

Sauté the seafood and vegetable in clarified butter and do not let it color. Season with salt, pepper and few drops of lemon juice.

Flame with half of the Vermouth and the white wine, remove and keep warm.

Reduce the other half of Vermouth by half in pan, add the fish veloute and simmer for a few minutes, season to taste.

Using a hand mixer, blend the cold butter to the sauce. Strain through a fine sieve and mix the whipped cream to the sauce.

Boil lasagne noodles in salted water until done. Place one layer on a dinner plate. Return seafood and vegetables to the sauce and bring to simmer until very hot.

Pour seafood onto lasagne and cover with another layer of noodle dough.

Serve right away.

Ingredients

Serves 2
3 cl clarified butter
50 g chopped shallots
120 g turbot fillet
120 g salmon fillet
100 g scallops
12 medium sized shrimp
120 g Dover sole
50 g carrot diamond
50 g leek diamond
50 g celery diamond
50 g white wine
10 cl Vermouth
1 dl fish veloute
20 g cold butter
8 piece lasagne noodles, 6 x 9 cm
salt, pepper, lemon juice
1 dl whipped cream

Recommended Wines

Robert Mondavi 1990 Fumé Blanc

Vichon 1991 Chevrignon

Bow-tie Pasta with Lobster & Artichokes

Chef Jamie Morningstar, Napa Valley, California

Ingredients

Serves 2
3 cups heavy cream
1 cup dry sherry
2 cups lobster meat, diced
1 cup artichoke hearts, diced
1 cup tomatoes, peeled, seeded and diced
1/2 cup scallions, chopped
salt, white pepper
4 cups bow-tie pasta, pre-cooked

Method

Reduce cream by half over low heat. At the same time, in a separate pan, cook the artichokes, tomatoes and lobster meat in the sherry.

Add the scallions at the last, along with the cream.

Season with salt, pepper.

Toss the pasta in hot water and drain well. Add to the lobster mixture and heat through.

Serve immediately.

Garnish with lobster claw and lemon wedge to side of pasta.

Recommended Wines

Vichon 1991 Chardonnay

Robert Mondavi 1991 Reserve Chardonnay

Petits Champignon

aux Fruits de Mer

Chef Minao Ishizaka, Caesar Park Ipanema, Rio de Janeiro

Method

Get the olive oil hot, fry garlic and onions first, then shrimp and scallops.

Soak Kikurage till soft, then chopped. Add mushrooms, chopped Kikurage.

Finish the sauce with cognac, white wine, chicken bouillon, soya sauce and coconut cream. Reduce.

Season with black pepper.

Recommended Wines

Vichon 1991 Chardonnay

Robert Mondavi 1991 Sauvignon Blanc

Ingredients

Serves 2
100 g garlic, chopped
1 onion, sliced thinly
1 dl olive oil
1 dl white wine
1 tsp black pepper
12 big shrimp
8 scallops
100 g Shimeji mushrooms
100 g Shiitake mushrooms
100 g Kikurage (Japanese mushrooms)
100 g Enok Dake mushrooms
3 dl chicken bouillon
soya sauce
parsley
100 ml fresh coconut cream
1 dl cognac

Garnish:
baby carrots, blanched
shrimp heads, blanched

Steamed Malabar Snapper

with Thai Basil Butter Sauce

Chef Mark Hellbach, The Westin Resort, Macau

Ingredients

Serves 2

160 g Malabar snapper fillet, skin off
50 g shallots, sliced thinly
5 cl white wine
2 cl white vinegar
2 cl fresh cream
30 g butter
50 g Thai basil, chopped
1 Tbsp tomato concasse
asparagus tips
broccoli, blanched
baby carrots, blanched
abalone mushrooms, chopped
salt, pepper
5 cl fish stock

Method

Season fish with salt and pepper.

Steam fish fillet with shallots, white wine and white vinegar.

Reduce stock with the fresh cream to half its original volume. Add the Thai basil, tomato concasse and season to taste, monté with butter.

Garnish plate with the vegetables and pineapple pilaf.

Serve fish with basil butter sauce.

Decorate with basil leaf.

Recommended Wines

Vichon 1991 Chardonnay

Robert Mondavi 1991 Fumé Blanc

Grilled Prawns with Tequila

and Nectarine Cream Sauce

Chef Jamie Morningstar, Napa Valley, California

Method

Clean prawns and marinate in olive oil with lavender and chervil.

Sauté shallots in butter until limp. Add the nectarines, lime juice and Tequila and bring to simmer. Reduce until nearly dry.

Add the cream and reduce by half until the sauce becomes the desired consistency. Whisk in the cumin.

Reserve in a warm water bath until needed.

Remove excess oil from prawns with fingers. Grill on skewers and serve with sauce ladled over.

Decorate with snow peas, cut ribbon edge and blanched vegetable concasse.

Ingredients

Serves 4
16 - 20 prawns, deveined
1 cup olive oil
1 tsp lavender, optional
1 tsp chervil, optional

Nectarine Sauce:
1 Tbsp butter
1 Tbsp shallots, roughly chopped
1 nectarine, finely diced
1 lime, juice only
1/2 cup Tequila
2 cups heavy cream
1 tsp cumin

Recommended Wine

Deinhard 1990 Riesling Dry

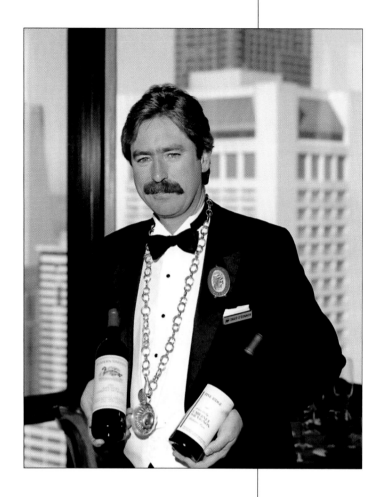

David O'Connor
Master Sommelier
*Victor's View, The Westin St Francis,
San Francisco*

One of the most respected authorities in the wine industry, David O'Connor has been the Sommelier at Victor's for the past 19 years, and became only the fourth American to be designated a Master Sommelier by London's prestigious Guild of Master Sommeliers in 1984.

The Guild of Master Sommeliers is a craftsman's guild of wine waiters established 1953 in London's Vintner's Hall under the patronage of the Wine and Spirit Association of Great Britain and the British Hotel and Restaurant Association. Its primary objective is to promote a wider interest in knowledge of and proper service of wine.

When O'Connor passed the Master Sommelier examination in 1984, 64 applicants from all over the world vied for 10 spots in the intensive five-day seminar. He is currently one of only 22 Master Sommeliers nationwide and 65 worldwide. O'Connor has since been appointed to the Court of Master Sommeliers, a position requiring his knowledge to prepare Master Sommelier candidates for the entrance exam and to administer the tests.

O'Connor is responsible for Victor's award-winning winelist and supervises a cellar with over 240 various wines balanced between classic French and California boutique wineries.

*The Westin St Francis,
San Francisco,
California, USA*

Soufflé of Crab
with Scallops in Strudel

Chef Hans Günter Harms, Hotel Vier Jahreszeiten, Hamburg

Method

With all ingredients for the soufflé, produce a farcé.

Fill in timbale and poach in bain marie until firm.

Blanch the spinach, spread with scallops farcé, add diced scallops and wrap in spinach leaves and strudel, fry in clarified butter.

Mix the ingredients for sauce together until smooth.

Put butter in a small saucepan, fish fumé, reduce, add champagne and cream double.

Serve the soufflé and scallops on champagne sauce and garnish with fresh vegetables.

Ingredients

Serves 2

Soufflé of Crab:
250 g fresh crab meat
3 dl whipped cream
4 pieces egg white
salt, pepper
lemon
sambal olek

Scallops in Strudel:
10 pieces scallops, diced
200 g scallops farcé
10 pieces large spinach leaves
strudel

Sauce:
2 dl champagne
2 dl fish fumé
2 dl cream double
200 g butter

Garnish:
garden vegetables

Recommended Wines

Deinhard 1990 Riesling Dry

Robert Mondavi 1991 Reserve Chardonnay

Tournedos de Thon au Gingembre

Chef Minao Ishizaka, Caesar Park Ipanema, Rio de Janeiro

Ingredients

Serves 2
1 kg tuna fish fillet

Marinade: (use only two-thirds)
1 dl soya sauce
2 dl white wine
2 dl mirin (Japanese sweet sake)
200 g sugar
olive oil
100g flour (for dusting only)

Sauce:
¹/₃ of the marinade
1 dl Grand Marnier
1 dl orange juice
1 dl Cognac

Garnish:
2 oranges
1 carrot
1 zucchini squash
2 g ginger, finely julienne

Method

Put tournedos of tuna in the marinade for ten minutes and then dust lightly with flour and grill each tournedos in olive oil.

Prepare the sauce in a saucepan; with the one third of marinade left, add Grand Marnier, Cognac, orange juice and reduce.

Add a little of the fish fumé and reduce.

Slice the ginger in a very fine julienne, dry well and fry in very hot oil.

Place on top of the tournedos.

Recommended Wines

Cape Mentelle 1989 Shiraz

Robert Mondavi 1991 Reserve Chardonnay

Steamed Snapper with Ginger Sauce

Chef Tylun Pang, The Westin Kauai, Hawaii

Method

Ginger Sauce:

Heat peanut oil until smoking.

Remove from heat and cool. Use whatever oil that remained in the pan. Over medium heat, quickly stir fry the ginger, garlic, Chinese parsley, green onions and rock salt. Add to the peanut oil and let stand at room temperature until use.

Steam snapper (seasoned with salt) carefully, do not overcook.

Stir fry the leeks julienne in peanut oil quickly and remove to platter.

Serve steamed snapper slices on stir fried leeks.

Spoon ginger sauce over fish and drizzle with soya sauce and garnish.

Ingredients

Serves 1
3 oz fresh snapper, sliced
2 oz leeks, julienne
1/2 Tbsp peanut oil
1/2 tsp soya sauce

Garnish:
carrot slices
red pepper slivers

Ginger Sauce:
1 1/2 tsp ginger, chopped fine
1/4 tsp garlic, chopped fine
1 1/2 Chinese parsley, chopped fine
1/4 tsp rock salt
2 oz peanut oil
1 Tbsp green onions, chopped fine

Recommended Wines

Robert Mondavi 1991 Reserve Chardonnay

Robert Mondavi 1991 Sauvignon Blanc

Pot au Feu of North Seafood

with Small Green Dumplings

Chef Hans Günter Harms, Hotel Vier Jahreszeiten, Hamburg

Ingredients

Serves 2
Pot au Feu:
10 pieces fillet of sole
300 g fillet of turbot
10 pieces scampi
400 g salmon fillet
8 dl fish stock
500 g chopped vegetables
salt, pepper

Dumplings:
3 large tomatoes
20 g red and green pepper kernels
300 g chou past
200 g leaf spinach
2 dl fish sauce
100 g butter
salt, pepper

Recommended Wines

Vichon 1991 Chardonnay

Vichon 1991 Chevrignon

Method

Pot au Feu:
Cut the fish in portions, poach it with the seafood and vegetables in fish stock.

Dumplings:
Blanch the spinach and mash it, mix all ingredients together and make small dumplings with a teaspoon and boil the dumplings in hot water.

Add to the pot au feu and serve in soup plate as shown. Garnish with small bouquet of salad.

Seared Red Snapper

with Thai Curry Sauce

Chef Tylun Pang, The Westin Kauai, Hawaii

Method

Sauté snapper in hot pan with peanut oil, skin side down until crisp. Cook on other side until done.

Reserve on side until sauce is ready.

Thai Curry Sauce:

Heat oil in sauce pan, add curry paste and cook until bubbly. Add coconut milk and bring to a boil.

Season with fish sauce and sugar, to suit taste.

Serve fish skin side up with curry sauce and garnish with fried pompadum and deep fried spinach leaves.

Ingredients

Serves 1

4 oz red snapper fillet (with skin on)

1 oz peanut oil

Thai Curry Sauce:

1 Tbsp Thai red curry paste

2 Tbsp oil

1 cup coconut milk

1 tsp Thai fish sauce (or soya sauce)

2 tsp palm sugar (or brown sugar)

Garnish:

spinach leaves, blanched

1 piece pompadum, deep fried

Recommended Wines

Christian Moueix 1988 Merlot

Cape Mentelle 1989 Shiraz

Grilled Salmon

with Chinese Pesto Sauce

Chef Mark Hellbach, The Westin Resort, Macau

Method

Grill two slices of salmon. When grilling the salmon slices, make sure they do not dry out by basting with some oil.

For sauce, mix all ingredients together and pound to a pesto, except spring onions.

Sauté the pounded mixture together in some oil, season to taste and remove quickly from heat.

Top sauce on salmon fillet and a little on to the plate.

Serve fish with the potato balls, grilled spring onions with carrots.

Ingredients

Serves 1
160 g Norwegian salmon, cleaned
150 g spring onions, chopped

Sauce:
80 g coriander, cleaned and chopped
150 g ginger, chopped
2 garlic, chopped
1 ¹/₂ dl lemon juice
1 ¹/₂ dl rice wine
³/₄ dl light soya sauce
10 g sugar
1 tsp Szechuan pepper (dried hot chillies), crushed
1 tsp ground black pepper
salt, pepper

Garnish:
3 golden fried potato balls
baby carrots, blanched

Recommended Wines

Deinhard 1990 Riesling Dry

Robert Mondavi 1991 Sauvignon Blanc

Broiled Sea Bass with Parsley Ravioli
(Served with California Vegetable Vinaigrette)

Chef Tadashi Katoh, Chef de Cuisine, Century Plaza Hotel, Los Angeles

Ingredients

Serves 2
4 pieces 6 oz sea bass
12 pieces parsley ravioli
3 oz peanut oil
1 oz sherry vinegar
4 pieces asparagus, sliced, cooked
4 pieces baby corn, sliced, blanched
2 Tbsp green cabbage, diced,
blanched
1 tsp pink peppercorn, crushed
2 tsp chives, chopped
2 Tbsp red cabbage, diced,
blanched
4 bunches cilantro leaves
4 oz *tomato coulis
salt, pepper

*Tomato Coulis:
5 oz canned tomato
1 oz Xeres vinegar
2 Tbsp orange juice
1/2 tsp sugar
salt, pepper

Parsley Ravioli:
2 oz parsley, blanched until soft
2 oz cream
salt, pepper, nutmeg
7 oz pasta sheet

Method

Tomato Coulis:
Place all ingredients in a mixer. Season with salt and pepper. Mix until soumieuse.

Parsley Ravioli:
Place the parsley, chopped and cream in pan. Reduce until all liquid is evaporated. Season with salt, pepper and nutmeg. Let cool.
Make ravioli about two inches round with pasta sheet.

Vegetable Vinaigrette:
Mix sherry vinegar, salt, pepper. Add peanut oil. Add the vegetables, chives, pink peppercorn and mix well.

Finally, season the sea bass with salt and pepper. Broil on both sides. Pour the vegetable vinaigrette in the middle of the plate. Put the broiled sea bass on top of it. Pour the tomato coulis on three points. Place the parsley ravioli. Decorate with cilantro between ravioli.

Recommended Wines
Vichon 1989 Chevrignon
Robert Mondavi 1991 Reserve Chardonnay

Pfannfisch Vier Jahreszeiten

Chef Hans Günter Harms, Hotel Vier Jahreszeiten, Hamburg

Method

Peel potatoes, slice into five millimetre slices, rinse in cold water.

Dry them, then fry them in clarified butter (golden). Sauté the diced onions in butter, mix them with the mustard.

Cut the turbot fillet into medallions.

Cut the potatoes, onions and turbot in layers, spice them with salt and pepper, lay them in a frying pan. Remove and bake them on a baking tray in the oven for 12 minutes.

Julienne Savoy cabbage, blanch them and cook in double cream, season with salt and pepper, add chopped chives and tomatoes concasse.

Serve Savoy cabbage on a plate and dress the pfannfisch on top of it.

Ingredients

Serves 2
500 g fillet of turbot
10 pieces large potatoes
2 pieces Savoy cabbage
4 dl double cream
200 g clarified butter
3 Tbsp German mustard
3 onions
4 tomatoes, concasse
1 bunch chives
salt, pepper

Recommended Wines

Deinhard 1990 Riesling Dry

Robert Mondavi 1990 Fumé Blanc

Caramelized Sea Scallops

in Truffle Sauce

Chef Tadashi Katoh, Chef de Cuisine, Century Plaza Hotel, Los Angeles

Ingredients

Serves 2
12 sea scallops, cut into half
2 oz port wine
1 oz veal stock
¹/₂ cup mussels stock
1 oz butter, unsalted
2 tsp chopped truffle
2 tsp truffle juice
1 Tbsp hazelnut oil
12 pieces baby carrots, glazed
4 oz spinach, sauteed with butter

Method

Flame the port wine and add the veal stock, mussels stock and bring to a boil and reduce by a third.

Monté with one ounce of butter and at the last moment, add the truffle juice and chopped truffles.

Sauté the scallops in hazelnut oil over high heat until golden brown in colour.

Arrange the garnish and scallops on a plate and pour the sauce on the plate.

Decorate with chervil.

Recommended Wines

Deinhard 1990 Riesling Dry

Robert Mondavi 1991 Reserve Chardonnay

Mango Creme Brulee
with Fresh Florida Strawberry Coulis

Chef Waldo Brun, Corporate Executive Chef, Walt Disney World Swan, Florida

Method

First, make the short dough by creaming the butter and sugar. Blend in eggs and the two flours. Refrigerate for two hours.

Now make the paté choux by bringing the milk, water and butter to a boil. Add the flour and blend until it comes together. Place in a 20 quart bowl with a paddle and blend in eggs and cinnamon.

Roll out the short dough to quarter inch and dock it. Now pipe a paté choux ring around the perimeter. Bake at 400 degrees Fahrenheit for 20 minutes.

Next bring to boil the cream, vanilla bean, lemon and one third of the sugar. Whip the eggs with the remaining sugar, then temper into the boiling cream, and whip until it boils again. Pour immediately into the pastry shell, then let cool for half hour.

Arrange mangoes over cream. Sprinkle with brown sugar and gratinee.

Serve with fresh strawberry coulis.

Ingredients

Serves 6
Short Dough Bottom:
1 lb sugar
2 lb butter
6 oz eggs
1 1/2 lb cake flour
1 1/2 lb high gluten flour

Cinnamon Paté Choux Sides:
1 pt milk
1 pt water
1 lb butter
1 lb 4 oz high gluten flour
1 qt eggs
2 oz cinnamon

Brulee Creme:
1 qt cream
10 oz sugar
10 each eggs
1 vanilla bean
2 mangoes

Strawberry/Mango Coulis:
the remaining mangoes and fresh strawberries

Recommended Wine

1983 Bernkasteler Doctor Riesling Auslese

Riesling-Raspberry Creme
in Terrine of "Baumkuchen"

Chef Hans Günter Harms, Hotel Vier Jahreszeiten, Hamburg

Method

Gelatine to be soaked in cold water until soft. Riesling, egg yolks and sugar should be beaten over a basin of hot water. When they are beaten, put the gelatine in and leave to cool.

Lastly, fold the whipped cream under.

Riesling-Raspberry Creme:
Soak gelatin in cold water, beat the egg yolks and raspberry concentrate over a basin of hot water, put in the gelatin and beat the mixture until cold.

Add the sweetened whipped cream and raspberry concentrate with the liqueur.

Terrine:
Cover the inside of a form with "Baumkuchen", fill with layers of Riesling-Raspberry Creme, cover it with "Baumkuchen", cool for approximately two hours. Then knock out of form and cut with warm knife into slices.

Ingredients

Serves 6
625 ml Riesling wine
250 g sugar
15 egg yolks
10 leaves of gelatin
750 g sweetened whipped cream

Riesling-Raspberry Creme:
600 g raspberry juice concentrate
15 pieces egg yolks
125 g raspberry concentrate
5 cl Himbeergeist (raspberry liqueur)
10 gelatin leaves
750 g sweetened whipped cream

Recommended Wine
1983 Bernkasteler Doctor Riesling Auslese

Quindao

(Quindinho)

Chef Fabiano Marcolini, Caesar Park Hotel, Sao Paulo

Ingredients

Serves 4
3 Tbsp butter
500 g sugar
1 coconut cream
10 egg yolks
2 whole eggs

Note: Fresh coconut cream can be obtained from freshly grated coconut. To obtain the cream, add two cups of water to the freshly grated coconut and squeeze till dry.

Method

Mix sugar with the butter until well mixed.

Add the ten egg yolks to the mixture above and mix well.

Pass the yolk mixture through a fine sieve and add two eggs to this mixture.

Add the coconut cream and mix well.

Prepare the individual moulds.

Put the egg mixture inside and cook in bain marie until firm.

Turn when the mould is still warm.

Recommended Wine

1983 Bernkasteler Doctor Riesling Auslese

La Petite Crepe Tropicale

Chef Minao Ishizaka, Caesar Park Ipanema, Rio de Janeiro

Method

Prepare avocado mousse by mixing pulp of the avocado and mangoes, chantilly, sugar and four gelatin leaves.

Put this mixture in the refrigerator to chill for two hours.

Prepare one crepe per person.

Crepe Batter:
Mix ingredients, slowly adding half litre of milk, until finished. Leave to stand for two hours at room temperature.

Using a crepe pan, prepare crepe and keep warm over a sauce pan of boiling water.

Serve one crepe of avocado mousse on a mango sauce. Garnish with fresh fruit as shown.

Ingredients

Serves 4
300 g pulp of avocado
300 g pulp of mango
300 g chantilly
300 g sugar
4 gelatin leaves

Crepe Batter:
250 g sifted flour
75 g superfine sugar
pinch of salt
3 eggs, beaten
1 egg yolk

Recommended Wine

1983 Bernkasteler Doctor Riesling Auslese

Green Tea Ice Cream with Sour Cream Compote

Chef Mark Hellbach, The Westin Resort, Macau

Ingredients

Serves 6
1 l milk
600 ml Swiss cream
140 g egg yolk (approx 20 pieces)
14 g sugar
40 g green tea powder
200 g eggs (approx 10 pieces)

Garnish:
600 g sour cherry compote
1 l whipped cream

Method

Pasteurize all ingredients in machine or cook to a rose.
Freeze in sorbetiere.

Arrange ice cream in a dish and decorate with cherries and whipped cream.

Recommended Wine
1983 Bernkasteler Doctor Riesling Auslese

Stolichnaya and Lime Sorbet

Chef Jamie Morningstar, Napa Valley, California

Method

In a medium size mixing bowl, combine all ingredients except the egg white and blend together. Pour into ice cream cannister and follow the manufacturer's direction for freezing. Transfer to a freezer container and freeze until firm.

Freezer Method:

Pour prepared mixture into several small containers suitable for freezing and cover with foil. Freeze in freezer until slushy. In a medium size mixing bowl, beat together the semi-frozen sorbet and egg white until light and smooth. Return to containers, cover and freeze until firm.

Garnish with lime juice and lime zest strips.

*Simple Syrup:

Combine all ingredients in a medium size saucepan and mix until all sugar is dissolved. Bring ingredients to a gentle boil over medium heat and simmer together for ten minutes. Remove from heat and cool before using. Can be stored in refrigerator in a covered container for two to three weeks.

Ingredients

Serves 6

$^1/_3$ *cup lime juice (about 2-3 limes)*
$^1/_4$ *cup lemon juice (about 2 lemons)*
*2 cups *simple syrup*
1 cup water
$^1/_4$ *cup tequila*
1 egg white, whipped (optional)

*Simple Syrup:

1 lb granulated sugar
2 cups water
zest from limes and lemons

Recommended Wine

1983 Bernkasteler Doctor Riesling Auslese

Hans Günter Harms
Chef
Hotel Vier Jahreszeiten, Hamburg

Hotel Vier Jahreszeiten,
Hamburg, Germany

"My kitchen philosophy consists of the preparation of seasonal and fresh products with emphasis on the Northern German region.

It is important to me to purchase as many ecologically grown ingredients and utilize them when fresh. Furthermore, it is my desire to work in harmony with nature, not to participate in the ruinous exploitation of our oceans and shores, keep close seasons, and not to use products which are under preservation or are endangered in their population.

It is important to me to impart and broaden our cooks' skill and their fundamental knowledge.

To achieve unique and well balanced dishes for my guests, the "à la minute" preparation is a matter of course.

The modification and revision of traditional as classical dishes and the creation of new dishes gives very much delight in my job.

The delight will double, if you, dear guests, have a pleasant culinary experience in our restaurant."

- culinary philosophy of Hans Günter Harms

Vanilla Ice Cream and California Fruit Trio

Chef Tadashi Katoh, Chef de Cuisine, Century Plaza Hotel, Los Angeles

Method

Remove stones from the poached peaches.

Arrange the orange wedges and cherries on a plate in a circle following the edge of the plate. Place a peach in the middle of the orange wedges and put the ice cream on top of the peach.

Sprinkle with orange zest over the oranges.

Pour orange juice over oranges.

Decorate with mint leaves.

Sprinkle chopped pistachio nuts on top of ice cream.

Ingredients

Serves 2
2 peaches, peeled, then vacuum-packed with sugar syrup and vanilla beans, cook in boiling water for ten minutes
6 oz vanilla ice cream
16 pieces oranges wedges in own juice, cooked with grenadine syrup
4 Tbsp orange zest
2 tsp chopped pistachio
4 mint leaves
6 pieces cherries, cut into half and remove stones
6 Tbsp orange juice

Recommended Wine

1983 Bernkasteler Doctor Riesling Auslese

Hamburger "Rote Grutze"

with Vanilla Flan

Chef Hans Günter Harms, Hotel Vier Jahreszeiten, Hamburg

Ingredients

Serves 4
Rote Grutze:
500 g red currant berries
500 g raspberries
500 g blackberries
500 g strawberries
40 g maizena (food starch)
40 g vanilla powder
1 bottle red wine
500 g sugar
2 lemons
1 dash salt
500 ml red fruit juice

Vanilla Flan:
250 ml milk
60 g sugar
4 pieces egg
1 piece vanilla pod

Method

Rote Grutze:
Cook all ingredients. When it starts to boil, add the vanilla power and the maizena, boil for ten minutes, strain through a fine sieve, fill it in portion and let it cool.

Vanilla Flan:
Cook the milk with the vanilla pod, pour it over eggs and sugar, strain it, fill it up in timbale and poach it 20 minutes by 80 degrees Fahrenheit.

Recommended Wine

1983 Bernkasteler Doctor Riesling Auslese

Egg White Pudding

Chef Fabiano Marcolini, Caesar Park Hotel, Sao Paulo

Method

Mix sugar and egg white together and cook in low heat until the sugar is dissolved until you don't feel the sugar granules in your fingers.

Remove from heat and at blend lowest speed until firm.

Pipe into the mould, which you will put dried fruit at the bottom and cook in bain marie at 120 degrees Celsius, for 30 minutes at the maximum.

Brush moulds with butter and sugar.

Baba de Mocca/Coconut Egg Sauce:
Boil the sugar until in low heat and add the yolks and coconut milk until the mixture curds.

Dissolve the coffee Nescafe, add to taste.

Beat in the liquid and leave to cool.

Ingredients

Serves 4
50 g dried fruits
1 kg sugar
1 ½ kg egg white

Baba de Mocca/Coconut Egg Sauce:
500 ml coconut milk
30 egg yolks
2.5 g Nescafe coffee
1 kg sugar
50 ml water

Recommended Wine

1983 Bernkasteler Doctor Riesling Auslese

Papo-de-Anjo

Chef Minao Ishizaka, Caesar Park Ipanema, Rio de Janeiro

Method

Beat the egg yolks up to the "ruban" and then add cornstarch.

Make syrup by boiling the water and the sugar, keep hot.

Cook in 20 very small timbales for 15 minutes at 180 degrees Fahrenheit.

Then put it in a hot sugar syrup and leave it for a few hours.

Serve with raspberry sauce and chantilly. Garnish as shown.

Ingredients

Serves 4
15 egg yolks
50 g cornstarch

Syrup:
500 g sugar
1 l water

Garnish:
raspberry sauce
chantilly

Recommended Wine

1983 Bernkasteler Doctor Riesling Auslese

SPIRIT OF
THE
SEASON

4 Spirit of
the Season

Soups

Appetizers

Main Courses

Salads

Desserts

Coffee

"Spirit of the Season"

*"Let us celebrate," was the theme of the poster;
highlighting a season of giving and traditions.
What a great way to end the year! Beautiful, traditional dishes
from various parts of the world, prepared by the best Master Chefs,
and paired with a great variety of wines - the new and old world.
The very special coffee recipes which rounded up this promotion because in most
locations, this year-end promotion was celebrated in the coldest season.
Perhaps among these recipes you will find flavors from your family's origins.
Celebrate with a recipe from your family's tradition.*

Menu Development Task Force

(left to right)

Andreas Knapp *Former Executive Chef, Food & Beverage Director,* Century Plaza Hotel & Tower
David C. Roveto *Vice President,* National Account Director, Fetzer Vineyards
Manfred Ochs *Executive Chef,* ANA Hotel, Washington D.C.
Tylun Pang *Executive Chef,* The Westin Kauai
Felix Subuyuj-Buccaro *Chef de Cuisine,* Camino Real, Guatemala City, Guatemala
Werner Glur *Executive Chef,* The Westin Bonaventure, Los Angeles
Roberto Iglesias *Executive Chef,* Camino Real, Guatemala City, Guatemala
Gerhardt Wind *Executive Chef,* The Westin Peachtree Plaza, Atlanta
Tadashi Katoh *Chef de Cuisine,* Century Plaza Hotel & Tower, Los Angeles
Rudolph Blattler *Executive Chef,* The Westin Harbour Castle, Toronto, Canada
Thierry Dufour *Executive Chef,* Camino Real, Cancun, México
Kurt H. Fischer *Vice President* Food & Beverage Division, Westin Hotels & Resorts

Additional Participants from Century Plaza Hotel & The Westin Bonvaventure:

Thomas Henzi, *Pastry Chef* **Simon Johns,** *Executive Sous Chef*
Alexander Purroy, *Sous Chef* **Hung Sik Shin,** *Second Commis*
Lou Cabales, *Apprentice* **Aram Scorza,** *Apprentice* **Chris Miehle,** *Apprentice*
Robert Urquidi, *Apprentice* **Frederick Book,** *Apprentice*
Richard Ramirez, *Sous Chef*

"Spirit of the Season"
List of Recipes

Soups

Appetizers

Main Courses

Coffees

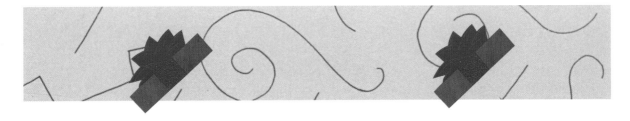

Oyster and Tofu Soup

Far East, Korea

Ingredients

Serves 4
4 doz oysters, shucked
1 ½ lb tofu, cut into one-inch pieces
4 oz fish stock or water
4 oz sake (Japanese rice wine)
6 oz miso paste
salt, pepper
green onions, chopped into two inch lengths

Method

Place the fish stock and sake into an earthen pot and bring to a boil.

Add miso paste and mix.

Add the tofu and simmer for two to three minutes.

Add the oyster and green onions and remove from the fire.

Serve immediately.

Season to taste.

Recommended Wines

Fetzer Barrel Select Sauvignon Blanc 1991

Fetzer Barrel Select Chardonnay 1991

Korean Rice Cake Soup (Duk Gug)

- special for New Year celebration

Far East, Korea

Method

Place bouillon in pot and bring to a boil.

Sauté the ground beef in a pan with some cooking oil. Add the sauteed ground beef and rice cake and cook for five minutes.

Place in a soup bowl and sprinkle with broken Nori seaweed and chopped green onions on top.

Serve immediately.

Ingredients

Serves 4
²/₃ lb rice cake
²/₃ qt beef bouillon
4 oz ground beef
1 sheet Nori seaweed, broken to pieces
1 Tbsp spring onions, chopped
cooking oil

Recommended Wines

Fetzer Barrel Select Sauvignon Blanc 1991

Fetzer Barrel Select Chardonnay 1991

Sam Kae Tang

(Young Chicken Soup with Ginseng)

Far East, Korea

Ingredients

Serves 2
250 g young chicken
20 g fresh ginseng
5 g jujube
3 g chestnut
20 g glutinous rice
5 g table salt
2 g ground white pepper
2 g Aji-no-moto (optional)
4 cloves garlic, crushed

Method

Remove chicken feet and wash.

Soak glutinous rice in water, drain.

Clean fresh ginseng.

Stuff chicken with glutinous rice, half of the garlic, jujube and fresh ginseng.

Tie the chicken with cotton twine to keep stuffing in.

Season with table salt.

Pour enough water in the saucepan to cover the chicken; add the rest of the garlic and boil thoroughly for two to three hours.

Add Aji-no-moto if you desire, at this stage.

When the chicken is done, serve in a bowl.

Garnish finely chopped green onions, salt and pepper.

Soup is usually served with rice and other Korean dishes.

Recommended Wines

Fetzer Barrel Select Chardonnay 1991

Robert Mondavi 1992 Chardonnay

Bulgogi with American Lamb

Far East, Korea

Method

Slice lamb loin into thin strips two to three inches in length. Take a bowl big enough to hold the lamb strips and add water, soya sauce, crushed and finely chopped garlic, thin slices of green onion, sesame seeds, Aji-no-moto, black pepper and sesame oil. Marinate the lamb in the mixture. The lamb is best cooked over charcoal but can be cooked under grill or in a frying pan over high flame.
To get an authentic taste of the dish, add a whole clove of garlic while cooking.
Serve with lettuce and green onion salad.

Green Onion Salad:

Cut green onions into two-inch lengths. Half them lengthwise and set aside to drain.
Mix powdered hot pepper, sugar, sesame seeds and sesame oil in soya sauce.
Mix the green onions with seasoning sauce. Serve in a bowl.
Mix green onion salad just before eating so that it will be fresh and not watery.
Eat with rice and other Korean side dishes.

Ingredients

Serves 2
21 oz American lamb loin
3 tsp sugar
3 tsp sake (Japanese rice wine)
3 tsp water
2 tsp garlic, crushed and finely cut
1 oz large onion, sliced thinly
2 tsp sesame seeds
6 tsp soya sauce
Aji-no-moto (flavoring, optional)
black pepper
sesame oil

Green Onion Salad:

3 oz green onions
a pinch of powdered hot pepper
¹/₄ tsp sugar
¹/₂ tsp sesame seeds
2 Tbsp sesame oil
¹/₄ tsp soya sauce

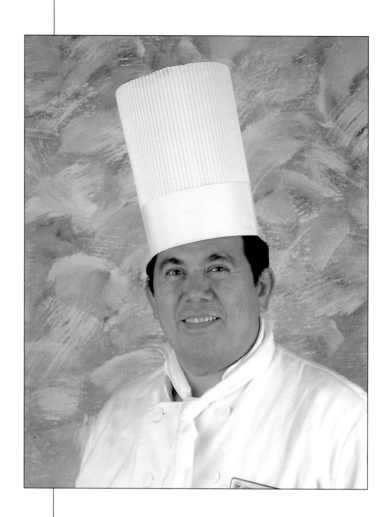

Roberto Iglesias

Executive Chef
Camino Real, Guatemala City

"To prepare distinctive dishes with great care and fondness which will add to the overall satisfaction of the client.

I prepare Kosher Buffets as well as Breakfast, Lunch and Dinner Buffets, all of them with a Guatemalan taste, combining high local quality products with excellent presentation including decorative ice, butter and chocolate sculptures.

I like to innovate both my dishes and their presentation because in the variety, you find the taste, the satisfied client and your own pleasure."

- culinary philosophy of Chef Roberto Iglesias

*Camino Real,
Guatemala City,
Guatemala*

Padd Thai

Stir Fried Thai Noodles

Far East, Thailand

Method

Heat wok or pan over high heat and add four tablespoons oil. Beat eggs quickly in a bowl. Pour in beaten eggs and fry very quickly, breaking the eggs up. Remove from heat.

Place four tablespoons of new oil in same pan and add the shrimp, garlic and let sweat for one minute.

Add the noodles, fried tofu and stir fry for one to two minutes.

Add garlic leaf, peanuts and season with red chilli, fish sauce, sugar, vinegar, sweat again for a few seconds.

Add the fried eggs and mix.

Place the noodles on plate and sprinkle with bean sprouts over the noodles.

Recommended Wines

Fetzer Barrel Select Sauvignon Blanc 1991

Fetzer Barrel Select Sauvignon Chardonnay 1991

Ingredients

Serves 4

18 oz rice noodles, soaked in hot water for ten minutes

8 Tbsp cooking oil

20 pieces shrimp, peeled

1 tsp garlic, finely chopped

2 oz garlic leaf or green onions cut into three-inch lengths

8 eggs

4 Tbsp peanuts, crushed

6 Tbsp fish sauce

2 Tbsp sugar

2 oz tofu, cut into quarter-inch strips, then fried

1 tsp red chilli, chopped

2 Tbsp vinegar or lemon juice

Garnish:

10 oz bean sprouts, cleaned, blanched

2 oz carrots, julienne

Bibimbap in Stone
(Mixed Rice with Vegetable and Meat)

Far East, Korea

Ingredients

Serves 4
100 g beef round, sliced
10 g green pea jelly, set
15 g bean sprouts, scalded
20 g Shiitake mushrooms, sliced
20 g Bellflower roots
20 g cucumber
15 g carrot
15 g spinach
1 egg, fried with sunny-side up
5 g ginkonuts
5 g chestnuts
5 g tangledried
5 g salt
10 g soya sauce
10 g sesame oil
8 cups steamed rice

Method

Season sliced beef and lightly stir fry in some oil until cooked.

Purée green pea jelly, mix the scalded bean sprouts with sesame oil; slice mushrooms - stir fry and season.

Scald the Bellflower roots and fry them with sesame oil and season.

Slice the cucumber, carrot and spinach.

Stir fry separately and season with soya sauce.

Boil tangledried and shred.

Place some steamed rice in a stone dish. Arrange all stir fried vegetables on top. Top with fried egg sunny-side up.

Sprinkle with gingkonuts and chestnuts.

Place dish topped with vegetables and meat in an open gas range until it is slightly burnt on top and serve.

Recommended Wines

Fetzer Barrel Select Chardonnay 1991

Fetzer Barrel Select Sauvignon Blanc 1991

Kalbi Gui Broiled Beef Ribs

Far East, Korea

Method

Remove meat from the bone and cut into strips.

Soak the strips of meat into a mixture of pear syrup, five grams sugar and half of the Japanese sake for ten minutes.

Mix together the soya sauce, sugar, sake, water, sliced onions, crushed garlic, sesame seeds, beer, white pepper and sesame oil.

Add the meat to the mixture and leave to marinate for one to two hours.

Remove meat from marinade and cook under a hot grill or fry in a pan.

Garnish and serve with rice and other Korean side dishes.

Ingredients

Serves 4
300 g short ribs
30 ml soya sauce
10 g sugar
5 g sesame seeds
30 ml Japanese sake
10 g garlic, crushed
5 g onions, sliced
10 g ground white pepper
15 ml pear syrup
30 ml beer
10 ml water
10 ml sesame oil

Recommended Wines

Fetzer Barrel Select Zinfandel 1989

Fetzer Valley Oaks Cabernet Sauvignon 1990

Nebiani

Broiled Beef Tenderloin

Far East, Korea

Ingredients

Serves 1
200 g beef tenderloin
5 ml of pear syrup
10 ml soya sauce
10 g sugar
2 g white pepper, ground
5 g green onions, sliced
5 g garlic, crushed
10 ml sesame oil
3 g pineapple
3 g pinenut powder
5 g sesame seeds

Method

Remove excess fat from tenderloin with knife and cut into pieces three centimeters or one inch thick.

Soak them in cold water for a while to remove blood.

Next, soak meat in a mixture of pear syrup, sugar, pineapple, pinenut powder, garlic, soya sauce, sliced green onions and sesame oil.

Season with white pepper to taste.

Roast the meat until done.

Sprinkle with sesame seeds before serving with rice and other Korean or Oriental dishes.

Recommended Wines
Fetzer Valley Oaks Cabernet Sauvignon 1990
Fetzer Barrel Select Zinfandel 1989

Sukiyaki

Far East, Japan

Method

Put the beef fat in a sukiyaki pan or iron pan and add the beef and sweat very quickly.

Add the beef bouillon and bring to a boil.

Season as you desire.

Arrange the other ingredients and cook for a few minutes as shown. Continue to add ingredients as required throughout the course of the meal.

Optional:
Dip vegetables, light soya sauce, fish gravy.

Cook rice or noodles together with sukiyaki in same pot.

Note: This is a tasty dish and has great entertainment value as well. Ingredients are usually served raw and arranged attractively. Guests can enjoy cooking their own food.

Ingredients

Serves 4
2 lb rib of beef, finely sliced
1 lb tofu, broiled both sides, then cut into one inch cubes
¹/₂ lb large green onion, sliced
4 oz burdock, finely julienne
¹/₂ lb vermicelli
2 package Enoki mushrooms, sliced
¹/₂ lb Shiitake mushrooms, sliced
¹/₂ lb Chinese cabbage, sliced
1 oz beef fat
16 oz mirin (Japanese sweet sake)
16 oz soya sauce (to mix with mirin above)
8 oz beef bouillon

Optional:
Udon noodles, rice cake, steamed rice

Recommended Wines

Robert Mondavi 1991 Pinot Noir

Fetzer Barrel Select Zinfandel 1989

Werner Glur
Executive Chef
The Westin Bonaventure,
Los Angeles

The Westin Bonaventure,
Los Angeles, California, USA

"I have devoted my professional career to giving pleasure to others through my culinary skills. I create all my menus around the freshest ingredients I can find during the seasons. The simplest methods of cooking bring out the natural flavor of a dish. Since eating is one of the basic joys of life, the ability to serve really good food is a gift I like to share with others".

- culinary philosophy of Chef Werner Glur

Werner Glur, Executive Chef of the Westin Bonaventure, is a well-known, award-winning culinarian.

Chef Glur has been with Westin Hotels & Resorts for over 24 years. Presently, as Executive Chef of The Westin Bonaventure, Glur supervises three kitchens and a staff of 58. He is responsible for the efficient and profitable functioning of all of the hotel's cooking facilities including the pastry shop.

In 1984, he was named Chef of the Year by the California Restaurant Writers Association. His keen competition included Wolfgang Puck of Spago's and other leading West Coast chefs. In 1985 he was named Chef of the Year by his peer group, The Chef's de Cuisine Association.

His numerous awards reflect over 20 years of experience in international cuisine.

Bonaventure is extremely pleased to have a Chef of such renown heading its culinary staff of professionals.

Chanko Nabe

Far East, Japan

Method

Place the stock and sake in earthen pot and bring to a boil.

Add the meat, seafood and vegetables; cook until done. Add tofu. Season with salt, soya sauce and miso paste.

Can be cooked: with Udon noodles, rice cake or steamed rice in same pot.

Serve condiments in separate small dishes with soup.

Note: This recipe may be used with any type of meats or vegetables or seafood to your preference.

Recommended Wines

Robert Mondavi 1991 Pinot Noir

Fetzer Barrel Select Chardonnay 1991

Ingredients

Serves 4
1 1/2 lb chicken meat, ground fine
1 tsp garlic, finely chopped
1 Tbsp miso paste
1 oz green onion, finely chopped
12 pieces shrimp
12 pieces scallops
12 pieces clams
1 lb Chinese cabbage, cut into two-inch pieces
1/2 lb Daikon radish
4 oz fried tofu, cut into cakes
4 oz Japanese sake
2 quart Bonito fish stock

Condiments:
sesame seeds, chopped
green onions, chopped
7 cayenne peppers
ginger, grated (optional)

Optional:
Udon noodles, rice cake, steamed rice

Enchiladas de Frijoles

Latin America, Guatemala

Ingredients

Serves 2
6 corn tortillas
8 Tbsp refried beans
2 Serrano chillies
1 green bell pepper
2 oz lard
grated Jack cheese

Method

Fry tortillas in lard.

Lay three of them on a plate with refried beans.

Make salsa out of chopped Serrano chillies. Spoon onto beans.

Sprinkle grated Jack cheese on them.

Garnish and serve.

Recommended Wines

Vichon 1990 Cabernet Sauvignon

Fetzer Valley Oaks Cabernet Sauvignon 1990

Tamales de Elote

Corn Tamales

Latin America, Guatemala

Method

Peel the corn trying to get complete leaves to wrap the tamales; then shell and grind the kernels.

Mix butter, sugar, ground cinnamon and egg yolks.

Add to ground corn.

If the dough is too dry, add enough milk to make into soft workable dough and a dash of baking powder.

Mix thoroughly.

Form small pieces of dough and wrap with corn leaves. Steam until done.

Dough will separate from leaf wrapping.

Ingredients

Serves 2
12 medium corn cobs, husks on
3 egg yolks
225 g butter
225 g sugar
1 cinnamon stick, finely ground
dash of baking powder
milk, as required

Tostadas Con Salsa

Latin America, Guatemala

Ingredients

Serves 2
8 corn tortillas
2 chilli pasilla, chopped
4 bell peppers, chopped
4 black peppercorns, ground
2 cloves garlic
2 oz lard
2 onions, finely chopped
1 achiote (smoked pablano pepper)

Garnish:
parsley, chopped
grated Jack cheese

Method

Fry the tortillas in lard lightly colored with achiote.

To make Salsa:
Lightly cook the chilli pasilla and bell peppers (deseeded) with ground peppercorn and cloves of garlic.
Add two finely chopped onions and continue cooking lightly.
Cover the tortillas with the salsa and top with chopped parsley and shredded cheese.

Recommended Wines

Fetzer Barrel Select Zinfandel 1989

Robert Mondavi 1991 Pinot Noir

Aquacate Relleno

(Stuffed Avocados)

Latin America, Guatemala

Method

Season and salt the asparagus spears, and sauté in some oil quickly. Put aside for garnish.

Peel avocados, cut in half, remove seeds and sprinkle with lemon juice and salt.

Finely dice chicken, ham and eggs; mix with two tablespoons of mayonnaise.

Add peas and chopped asparagus.

Stuff avocados with mixture and chill thoroughly before serving.

Ingredients

Serves 2
2 large avocados
1 chicken breast
2 Tbsp mayonnaise
2 oz ham
2 hard boiled eggs
¹/₂ cup cooked peas
3 asparagus spears, chopped
salt, to season

Garnish:
8 asparagus spears
enough oil for sauté
1 red pepper, cut into thin strips

Recommended Wines

Fetzer Barrel Select Chardonnay 1991

Fetzer Barrel Select Sauvignon Blanc 1991

Gerhardt Wind

Executive Chef
The Westin Peachtree Plaza,
Atlanta

The Westin Peachtree Plaza,
Atlanta, Georgia, USA

"Whether the food is prepared by the Executive Chef of a Five Star Hotel or the Weekend 'backyard cook', food and its preparation is an expression of art. The artist should experiment with recipes and add their own options that cater to their individual likes and dislikes. There is no one-and-only correct way to prepare a dish.

The basic rule of food and wine pairing is to attain a balance between the acids and sugars. People should experiment with these pairings and not be tied to convention. We need to be unbiased and maintain an open mind in order to appreciate the flavor of both the food and wine and to be aware of how each of their qualities enhance each other".

- culinary philosophy of Chef Wind

Executive Chef Gerhardt Wind has been with The Westin Peachtree Plaza since 1983. As Executive Chef of this 1,068 room hotel, Chef Wind is responsible for the total food and beverage operations of the hotel's four lounges and three restaurants and all catering functions. Chef Wind oversees a staff of 200 employees and 13 managers, serving an average of 2,000 plus meals daily.

Chicken Tamales

Latin America, Guatemala

Method

Cook the chicken pieces in the water until stock is obtained and chicken can be shredded. Shred chicken finely.

Mix corn flour, lard, baking powder and enough chicken stock to make lightly firm dough.

Season to taste.

Add shredded chicken to dough, wrap completely and firmly in corn husk leaves.

Place in a casserole, cover and steam cook for about forty minutes. When the dough is hard, it is done.

Beef, fish or shrimp can be substituted for the chicken.

Ingredients

Serves 5
1 kg freshly ground corn flour
250 g lard
4 Tbsp baking powder
1 ¹/₂ chickens, cut up
corn husk leaves, enough for wrapping
salt, pepper, to taste
5 l water

Recommended Wines

Fetzer Barrel Select Sauvignon Blanc 1991

Robert Mondavi 1991 Pinot Noir

Pozole

Pork and Hominy Soup

Latin America, submitted by The Westin Bonaventure

Ingredients

Serves 10
1 whole chicken (about 3 lb, cut up)
$^{1}/_{2}$ onion, sliced
3 cloves garlic, crushed
4 tsp salt
1 sprig cilantro (coriander)
24 cups cold water
2 lb boneless lean pork
1 lb boneless pork leg
2 lb dried hominy, cooked and drain

Condiments:

3 oz dried oregano
1 cup chopped green onions
3 oz ground chilli
5 limes, quartered

Method

Place the chicken in a large pot or Dutch oven and add onion, garlic, one teaspoon of salt and the cilantro. Cover with ten cups of water, bring to a boil and simmer, covered over medium heat for twenty minutes or until the chicken is tender. Transfer chicken to a plate, remove skin and bones and shred meat. Reserve the stock. There should be about eight cups.

Place the pork, pork leg and remaining salt in a large pot and cover with 14 cups water. When water comes to a boil, skim the surface and cook over medium heat for one hour. Add hominy and cook another 30 minutes. Remove and shred the meat and return it to the pot.

Add the chicken stock and shredded chicken to the pot, correct the seasonings, cover and cook over medium heat for 20 minutes or until the hominy is tender.

Serve in small soup bowls and pass separate dishes containing the oregano, chopped green onions, ground chilli and lime quarters.

Recommended Wines

Robert Mondavi 1991 Sauvignon Blanc

Fetzer Barrel Select Chardonnay 1991

Vallarta

(Green Seafood Soup)

Latin America, Mexico

Method

Prepare the stock using water, fish head, whole fish tail, glass of white wine and vegetables. Cook slowly over a low flame, strain the stock and separate the vegetables.

Blend the vegetables and mix in with the stock and keep warm.

Prepare the sauce; grind the chilli, parsley, coriander, "epazote", onions and garlic with three cups of the stock.

Heat in casserole, the oil and butter add the sauce and cook until it thickens.

Add the shrimp and season with salt and pepper.

Serve hot with lemon halves.

Recommended Wines

Fetzer Barrel Select Chardonnay 1991

Fetzer Barrel Select Sauvignon Blanc 1991

Ingredients

Serves 10

Broth:

1 l water
1 fish head, cleaned
1 whole fish tail, without meat
1 glass dry white wine
1/2 leek, sliced
1 turnip, sliced
1/2 garlic head, crushed
1 onion, sliced
10 bunch parsley, chopped
4 bay leaves
2 carrots, diced

Salsa:

6 diced chilli poblanos without seeds and skin
2 cups parsley, chopped
1/2 cup coriander, chopped
1/2 cup diced "epazote"
1/2 cup diced onions
1/2 garlic head
1/3 olive oil
10 g butter
20 shrimp

Red Snapper in Poblano Sauce

Latin America, Mexico

Ingredients

Serves 1
200 g red snapper fillet
200 ml fish stock
50 ml cream
60 g chilli poblano without seeds and skin, sliced
50 g butter
20 g potatoes
20 g carrots, julienne
20 g zucchini, diced freely
5 g fennel sprigs

Method

Blanch the finely diced zucchini. Put aside for garnish. Slice the potatoes in the form of scales and sauté with a little butter.

Decorate the fillet with the potatoes and sauté in a wide frying pan.

To make the sauce; blend the fish stock with the cream and the chilli poblano. Place the sauteed fish fillet with the "scaled" potatoes on top and surround it with the sauce and vegetables.

Garnish with fennel and blanched zucchini.

Recommended Wines

Fetzer Barrel Select Sauvignon Blanc 1991

Robert Mondavi 1992 Chardonnay

Bacalao a la Mexicana

(Dried Cod Mexican Style)

Latin America, Mexico

Method

Cover the cod in cold water and soak for twelve hours, changing the water two or three times, drain. Place in a saucepan, cover with water and bring just to a boil. Drain, remove the skin and bones, shred the flesh and set aside.

Remove the stem and seeds from the chilli ancho and soak in hot water for ten minutes. Drain, then purée in a blender with tomatoes and strain.

Heat the oil in a large skillet, add the onion and garlic and sauté until transparent. Add the purée and cook over low heat until it thickens. Add the cod, bay leaf, cinnamon, pepper, red peppers, almond, raisins, olives, capers and parsley. Stir, then cook over medium heat, covered for fifteen minutes. Add the potatoes, cover and cook over high heat for ten more minutes to heat through. Add salt if required.

Garnish with chilli Gueros.

Ingredients

Serves 4
2 lb dried salt cod
chilli ancho, roasted
2 lb tomatoes, diced
$^1/_2$ cup olive oil
1 large onion, finely chopped
6 cloves garlic, finely chopped
1 bay leaf
pinch ground cinnamon
pinch freshly ground pepper
1 seven oz jar roasted red peppers
$^1/_2$ cup sliced blanched almonds
$^1/_4$ cup raisins
$^1/_2$ cup pimiento-stuffed olives
2 Tbsp capers (optional)
2 Tbsp chopped parsley
1 lb small potatoes, cooked and peeled
salt (optional)
1 can chilli Gueros

Recommended Wines

Robert Mondavi 1992 Chardonnay

Fetzer Barrel Select Chardonnay 1991

Manfred Ochs
Executive Chef
ANA Hotel, Washington DC

"All the experience I have acquired in Europe, North America, and the Far East has given me the opportunity to create my own style of cooking, combining different techniques and seasonings with the freshest of produce now available in the United States.

I strongly believe in training culinary apprentice programs. It is the only way our industry will prosper in the future. Chefs should also share information and learn from each other. The days of having secret recipes are over."

- culinary philosophy of Chef Manfred Ochs

Manfred Ochs was born in Michelbach, Germany.

He joined Westin Hotels & Resorts in 1984 at their Edmonton Hotel, where he served as Executive Chef. During his tenure in Canada, Chef Ochs won an individual Gold Medal at the Culinary Olympics in Frankfurt, Germany and with the Canadian team he won a Gold Medal in Singapore. He also captured a Gold Medal in the World Culinary Art Festival in Vancouver.

In 1992, Manfred Ochs was named **The Chef of the Year** by the American Culinary Federation.

ANA Hotel,
Washington, DC, USA

Torta de Romeritos con Camarones

Latin America, Mexico

Method

Clean the Romeritos and boil in salted water for two minutes. Drain well and chop.

Dice shrimp and mix with eggs, cheese and Romeritos.

Heat corn oil in a casserole until very hot, and fry the shrimp mixture patted into round patties (cake-like) and set aside.

Put in a blender, the tomato, garlic and onion. Fry this mixture and add to the chicken stock. Season with salt and pepper.

When the stock is boiling add the shrimp patties and leave for two minutes, then serve in a bowl with lots of stock.

Ingredients

Serves 4
500 g Romeritos (fresh)
500 g cooked shrimp
125 g dry cheese (grated)
6 whole eggs
300 ml corn oil
4 tomatoes, roasted, seeded
2 cloves garlic, crushed
¹/₂ white onion, sliced
400 ml chicken
salt, pepper
parsley, sprigs

Recommended Wines

Fetzer Barrel Select Chardonnay 1991

Fetzer Barrel Select Sauvignon Blanc 1991

Guajolote en Mole Rojo

Latin America, Mexico

Ingredients

Serves 10
1 turkey (5 kg)
2 onions, sliced
1 head garlic, chopped
200 g chilli mulato
200 g chilli ancho
15 tomatillos
100 g sesame seeds
125 g sliced almonds
35 g chocolate
3 g ginger, julienne
25 g pumpkin seeds
20 black peppercorns
7 cloves
1 piece day-old bread
100 g lard
2 l chicken stock
1 bouquet garni

Garnish:
10 baby carrots, blanched
10 pieces zucchini, blanched
sprigs of parsley
steamed rice

Method

Roast and devein the chillies. Fry them in lard with sesame and pumpkin seeds, ginger, spices, sliced bread, roasted tomatillos and chocolate; stirring constantly to avoid burning.

Blend this a little at a time adding stock to make a fine paste (salsa). Return to stove in a casserole with stock until it begins to thicken, moving constantly and season with salt.

The turkey is cut up in pieces and boiled with the bouquet garni, two onions and a head of garlic. Once that is cooked, mix with the salsa. Bring it to boil slowly for seven minutes. Sprinkle sesame seeds on salsa.

Serve with small helping of white steamed rice as shown.

Recommended Wines
Fetzer Barrel Select Zinfandel 1989
Fetzer Barrel Select Cabernet Sauvignon 1989

Gallino en Pepian Mestizo

Latin America, Guatemala

Method

Boil the chicken in some water under medium heat until soft. Shred the chicken meat into small pieces.

Toast pumpkin seeds, sesame seeds, bell pepper, tomatillos and blend with the toasted French bread.

Fry toasted seeds mixture in lard.

Add salt and pepper and cilantro.

Add chicken stock and pieces of chicken.

Allow to stand before serving.

Serve with steamed rice.

Ingredients

Serves 4
1 chicken (approx 1 kg)
2 oz pumpkin seeds
1 oz sesame seeds
4 oz tomatillos
1 loaf French bread, toasted
1 bell pepper
1 sprig cilantro, chopped
lard
4 cups steamed rice
12 small pieces cucumbers, blanched
sprigs of parsley

Recommended Wines

Fetzer Barrel Select Cabernet Sauvignon

Robert Mondavi 1991 Pinot Noir

Cordero en Adobo

Latin America, Guatemala

Ingredients

Serves 8
3 lbs lamb loin, sliced lengthwise
very thin
salt, to taste
4 Tbsp vinegar
white pepper, ground
$^1/_2$ lb tomatillos
2 bell peppers
1 achiote
$^1/_2$ head garlic
2 onions, sliced
1 tsp oregano
$^1/_2$ tsp cominos
6 cloves, ground
1 stick cinnamon (small), ground
10 peppercorns, ground

Garnish:
28 pieces sauteed spring onions,
(without green part)
16 pieces corn chips
shredded mixed vegetables, sauteed

Method

Marinate the lamb loin with salt, vinegar and ground white pepper for 24 hours, turning every three hours.

Then grind the rest of the ingredients and thickly coat with marinated meat. Dry in the sun.

Fry or grill the meat. Serve with spring onions, corn chips and shredded mixed vegetables.

Recommended Wines

Robert Mondavi 1991 Pinot Noir

Fetzer Barrel Select Zinfandel 1990

Carne Envuelta en Huevo

Latin America, Guatemala

Method

Cut the boiled meat in slices. Add the juice of lemon and salt.

Whip eggs and flour and salt. Coat the meat and sauté in lard.

Make salsa by blending tomatoes, onions and tomatillos. Season to taste.

Ingredients

Serves 4
2 lbs top sirloin, boiled
3 eggs
4 oz lard
1 Tbsp flour
6 tomatoes
3 tomatillos
1 onion, sliced
1 juice of lemon
salt

Garnish:
pieces of baby carrots, blanched
pieces of zucchini, blanched
4 cups of steamed rice

Recommended Wine

Fetzer Valley Oaks Cabernet Sauvignon 1990

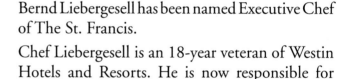

Bernd Liebergesell

Executive Chef
St Francis Hotel, San Francisco

Bernd Liebergesell has been named Executive Chef of The St. Francis.

Chef Liebergesell is an 18-year veteran of Westin Hotels and Resorts. He is now responsible for managing The St. Francis' kitchens and directing all aspects of food preparation and presentation.

Liebergesell has been honored as a Chef Rotisseurs of the Chaine des Rotisseurs; Certified Executive Chef, American Culinary Federation; Member, Pittsburgh's Culinary Olympic Team, and past Board Member of the Chefs and Cooks Association of the Pacific Coast. An active member of the San Mateo County Chefs Apprenticeship Program, he is a five-year member of the Academy of Westin Hotels Master Chefs, and has received two gold, two silver, and two bronze medals from the American Culinary Federation Culinary Arts Saloon since 1983.

St Francis Hotel,
San Francisco, California, USA

186

Pollo en Jugo en Naranja

(Chicken in Orange Juice)

Latin America, Mexico

Method

Clean chickens well and half them. Then sauté in butter until cooked through.

When evenly browned, add the onions, salt and pepper, bay leaves, thyme and the juice of the oranges.

Cover and cook slowly until done.

Serve with the thick sauce poured over chicken pieces.

Ingredients

Serves 4
2 spring chickens, approx 500 g each
60 g butter
4 sweet oranges, halved
2 onions, sliced
2 bay leaves
1 sprig thyme, chopped
salt, pepper

Recommended Wines

Fetzer Barrel Select Sauvignon Blanc 1991

Robert Mondavi 1992 Chardonnay

Hanukkah Potato Cakes

North America

Ingredients

Serves 4
2 large potatoes, peeled and grated
2 egg whites
1 white onion, grated fine
1 Tbsp flour
1 tsp baking powder
salt, pepper
2 Tbsp chopped chives
2 large potatoes, cut like
matchsticks

Method

Deep fry the julienne potatoes. Put aside for garnish. Peel potatoes and grate fine. Place grated potato into sieve and wash until water runs clear. Drain well. Combine in a bowl: grated potatoes, grated onion, flour and baking powder.

Whip up egg whites and fold under potato mixture.

Season well with salt and pepper, add chives.

Garnish with deep fried julienne potatoes.

Recommended Wines

Fetzer Barrel Select Sauvignon Blanc 1991

Fetzer Barrel Select Chardonnay 1991

Scottish Smoked Salmon

with Puff Pastry and Watercress Cream Sauce

North America

Method

Slice puff pastry triangles in half.

Sauté smoked salmon lightly and place on bottom of triangle.

Sauté spinach and oyster mushrooms, and place in center of salmon. Place triangle top on dish.

Add watercress sauce around puff pastry.

*Watercress Sauce:

Cook watercress in boiling water quickly, cool in iced water.

Reduce cream in a saucepan to half, cool.

Mix watercress and cream. Blend until smooth.

Season with salt, pepper and herb vinegar to suit taste.

Garnish with salmon caviar if desired.

Ingredients

Serves 3

12 oz Scottish smoked salmon
9 puff pastry triangles, cooked
4 oz spinach, blanched
8 oz *watercress sauce
4 oz oyster mushrooms
salmon caviar, if desired

*Watercress Sauce:

5 oz watercress
1 1/4 fl oz herb vinegar
7 fl oz cream
salt, pepper

Recommended Wines

Fetzer Barrel Select Sauvignon Blanc 1991

Fetzer Barrel Select Chardonnay 1991

Quinoa Waffle with Three Caviar

North America

Ingredients

Serves 4
for the waffle:
³/₄ cup sifted flour
³/₄ cup pre-cooked quinoa grains
1 egg
1 egg yolk
1 cup heavy cream
¹/₂ cup milk
2 Tbsp chopped chives
4 Tbsp melted butter

for garnish:
chives, chopped
2 oz Beluga Mandarin caviar
1 ¹/₂ oz salmon caviar
1 oz golden caviar
¹/₂ cup sour cream

for stuffing:
¹/₂ oz Beluga Mandarin caviar
1 Tbsp chopped egg yolk
1 Tbsp chopped egg white
1 Tbsp red onions, finely chopped
1 Tbsp chives, chopped
juice of half lemon
1 Tbsp olive oil
12 fresh cherry tomatoes
salt, pepper

Method

Place the flour and pre-cooked quinoa grains in a bowl.

In another bowl, beat together the egg and egg yolk. Add the cream, milk and chives to the egg mixture. Whisk the egg mixture into the quinoa grains and flour.

Whisk in the melted butter. Season to taste.

Heat waffle iron and spray with vegetable shortening. Divide batter evenly, close the waffle iron and bake for three to five minutes. After baking, take out the waffle and break into four pieces. Pipe a little sour cream into empty diamonds and fill up with different caviar on top.

Decorate waffle with chopped chives.

for stuffing:
Cut off the top of each tomato and remove the pulp. Mix all ingredients very gently together and season to taste. Fill tomatoes.

Serve three tomatoes with each waffle.

Recommended Wine

Robert Mondavi 1992 Chardonnay

Maryland Steamed Seafood Custard

North America

Method

for Vegetable Stock:

Heat two tablespoons oil in pan. Fry the onions and leeks until golden, then add the garlic. When the aroma rises, add tomatoes and cook for two minutes. Add thyme, bay leaf, fennel, carrots, celery and orange peel.

Pour in the boiling chicken stock and raise the heat to high. Season with salt and pepper and add saffron. Reduce heat and simmer for five to eight minutes.

Strain the stock through a sieve and cool.

Reserve the vegetables julienne for later use.

for Custard:

Mix the eggs lightly in a small bowl so that mixture does not become frothy. Stir in the vegetable stock.

Divide the scallops, shrimp, lobster, crab meat and julienne of vegetables among four soup plates and sprinkle with Daikon sprouts. Pour the egg mixture over the ingredients on the plates. Cover each plate with a lid or plastic wrap and steam in preheated steamer over medium heat for 15 minutes until the custard set; it should be soft. Serve very hot.

Ingredients

Serves 4
2 oz sea scallops
4 pieces fresh shrimp
2 oz jumbo lump crab meat
4 oz lobster tail meat
1/2 packet Daikon sprouts

for Custard:
4 eggs
3 cups *vegetable stock

*for Vegetable Stock:
2 oz olive oil
2 cloves garlic, chopped
1 large onion, chopped
1 leek, white part only, julienne
1/2 lb ripe tomatoes, peeled and chopped
1 carrot, julienne
1 stalk celery, julienne
1 sprig thyme
1/2 bay leaf
1/2 piece fennel, julienne
1 piece dried orange peel, julienne
1 1/2 pt chicken stock
1/8 tsp saffron

We are an environmentally and socially-conscious grower, producer and marketer of wines of the highest quality and value.

Working in harmony and with respect for the human spirit, we are committed to sharing information about the enjoyment of food and wine in a lifestyle of moderation and responsibility.

Multi-colored Garden Greens

with Basil Vinaigrette

North America

Method

for Basil Vinaigrette:

Blend Kresse vinegar, chopped red onions and chopped basil in a bowl.

Whisk in sunflower oil, season with crushed black pepper and salt.

Arrange the salad as shown, with tomatoes sprinkled around.

Ingredients

Serves 1
1 Oakleaf leaf
1 Belgian Endive leaf
1 Lollo Rosso leaf
1 Shiitake mushroom, sliced
1 Dandelion
2 Tbsp Daikon sprouts
1 tomato, diced finely
2 Romaine lettuce leaves
2 Boston lettuce leaves

for Basil Vinaigrette:
500 ml sunflower oil
150 ml Kresse vinegar
50 g chopped red onions
15 g chopped basil
10 g crushed black pepper
salt to taste

Recommended Wine

Fetzer Barrel Select Sauvignon Blanc 1991

Gravlax with Sweet Mustard Sauce

and Smoked Trout Dumplings

North America

Ingredients

Serves 4
4 Frisee leaves
4 Belgian endive leaves
300 g *smoked trout dumplings
12 slices gravlax
4 sprigs fresh dill
30 ml **sweet mustard sauce
1 tsp glace de viande

Smoked Trout Dumplings:
300 g smoked trout fillets
70 g cream cheese
juice of one lemon
2 Tbsp chives, chopped
salt, pepper
Worchestershire sauce
Tabasco

****Sweet Mustard Sauce:***
100 g Grey Poupon Dijon mustard
10 g sugar
5 Tbsp honey
3 egg yolks
3 tsp rice vinegar
500 ml olive oil

Method

Smoked Trout Dumplings:
Purée trout fillets and pass through fine chinoise. Combine with cream cheese and lemon juice. Adjust seasoning and add chives. Shape into dumplings with hot spoons.

****Sweet Mustard Sauce:***
Combine Grey Poupon Dijon mustard, egg yolks, honey, vinegar and sugar. Mix oil in last to emulsify.

Place three gravlax rosettes and one smoked trout dumpling on each plate. Arrange salad on plate as shown. Then spoon sweet mustard sauce onto front of the plate and make three lines from left to right with glace de viande (warm) through the sauce. With the tip of a skewer, pull through the three lines every inch to create a webbed effect.

Recommended Wines
Fetzer Barrel Select Chardonnay 1991

Robert Mondavi 1992 Chardonnay

Northern Ontario Bitter Leaf

with Beet and Truffle Vinaigrette

North America

Method

*Truffle Vinaigrette:

Chopped truffles very fine. Put all other ingredients in a bowl except the oils, vinegar and truffle juice.

Slowly add the oils, vinegar and truffle juice, gently blending the ingredients.

Season to taste with salt and pepper.

Arrange salad as shown, featuring a small piece of goat cheese and the beet pieces.

Surround the arrangement with the vinaigrette.

Recommended Wines

Fetzer Barrel Select Zinfandel 1989

Fetzer Barrel Select Cabernet Sauvignon 1989

Ingredients

Serves 4

1 leaf Belgian endive

1 leaf Red Oak lettuce

1 leaf Romaine lettuce

1 cucumber, hollowed

50 g goat cheese, in circles

20 g alfalfa sprouts

20 slices red beet

200 ml *truffle vinaigrette

*Truffle Vinaigrette:

50 g truffles

50 ml truffle juices

25 ml olive oil

25 ml sunflower oil

20 ml Kresse vinegar

20 ml Balsamic vinegar

30 g parsley, chopped

15 g fresh basil, chopped

2 medium red onions

2 cloves minced garlic

30 g Grey Poupon Dijon mustard

10 ml Worchestershire sauce

salt, freshly ground black pepper

Ukranian Borscht

North America

Ingredients

Serves 10
3 l beef stock
600 g white cabbage
200 g carrots
60 g potatoes
300 g raw beetroot
200 g leeks, peeled
200 g onions, peeled
200 g turnip, peeled
200 g celery
20 g parsley
200 g diced tomato concasse
bouquet garni

Garnish:
250 g sour cream
100 g raw beetroot

Method

Wash all vegetables. Peel. Chop onions and parsley. Cut other vegetables into strips.

Put beef stock in large pot. Add vegetables, except tomato concasse and bouquet garni.

Reserve small amount of beetroot for color.

Bring to boil. Cover. Simmer for 30 minutes.

Add tomatoes. Simmer for another 30 minutes.

Grate rest of beet root. Add to soup ten minutes before serving. Garnish with sour cream and celery leaf.

*Note: To get the string effect of sour cream in the soup, use piping tools.

Recommended Wines

Fetzer Barrel Select Zinfandel 1989

Robert Mondavi 1992 Pinot Noir

Crab and Brie Soup

North America

Method

Sauté the chopped white onions and celery in the unsalted butter for ten minutes.

Add flour slowly to avoid lumps, mix well.

Add seafood stock and bring to a boil for ten minutes.

To this, add the cream to your liking, crab meat and brie cheese. Simmer for another ten minutes.

Season with cajun seasoning and Worchestershire sauce to taste.

Garnish with green onions. Soup will be slightly spicy hot.

Ingredients

Serves 10
1/2 lb white onions, chopped
1/2 lb celery, chopped
6 oz green onions, chopped
3 oz unsalted butter
3 oz flour
2 pt seafood stock
1 pt 35% cream
1/2 lb crab meat, chopped fine
2 lb brie cheese, cut up
cajun seasoning, to taste
Worchestershire sauce, to taste

Recommended Wines

Robert Mondavi 1992 Chardonnay

Fetzer Barrel Select Chardonnay 1991

Otto Weibel
Director of Kitchens
The Westin Stamford & Westin Plaza,
Singapore

The Westin Stamford & Westin Plaza,
Singapore

"My philosophy is to use only the freshest and best quality ingredients and prepare them in a simple way to bring out the natural flavour. Using the right basic preparation in accordance with modern cooking principles is also very important to me as this will give the food a natural and appetizing appearance.

All starches and ingredients should harmonize with the main item in terms of quantity, taste and colour and should correspond to modern nutritional theory. Food preparation must be practical and food should be easily digestible.

Dining should be an experience of joy, happiness and entertainment."

- culinary philosophy of Chef Weibel

South Carolina Corn Chowder

North America

Method

In a soup pot, brown bacon, add the onions and sauté them for several minutes, do not brown the onions. Add the garlic and sauté all three ingredients a few minutes more.

Add the diced green and red pepper, the finely diced Idaho potatoes and the paprika powder. Sauté the celery, peppers and potatoes a little more. Mix in flour, add bay leaf, and chicken stock.

Bring the corn chowder to a boil and cook for 15 minutes. Add the kernel corn and simmer the corn chowder 15 minutes more.

Taste the chowder for flavor, add cream and parsley and do not boil the soup anymore. However, serve the soup very hot.

Ingredients

Serves 10
¹/₂ lb bacon, finely chopped
2 cups onions, finely chopped
6 cloves garlic, chopped finely
1 cup green celery, finely diced
¹/₂ cup red pepper, finely diced
¹/₂ cup green pepper, finely diced
2 Tbsp flour
bay leaf
1 lb fine kernel corn
3 qts chicken stock
1 qt light cream
4 Tbsp parsley, chopped
salt, ground white pepper
3 Idaho potatoes, finely diced
1 tsp paprika powder

Recommended Wines

Fetzer Barrel Select Sauvignon Blanc 1991

Fetzer Barrel Select Chardonnay 1991

San Francisco Fisherman's Wharf Cioppino

North America

Ingredients

Serves 4
24 Littleneck clams
1 1/2 lb halibut, cut into bite size pieces
16 shrimp, peeled and deveined
16 oysters, without shells
4 onions, diced
4 garlic cloves, crushed
3 oz olive oil
24 oz Italian plum tomatoes
18 oz tomato purée
8 oz Burgundy wine
10 oz fish stock
salt, pepper
8 Tbsp basil, majoram, oregano, rosemary mix
4 salmon fillets (7 oz each)

Method

Sauté onions and garlic, add Italian plum tomatoes, tomato purée and half of herbs in olive oil. Add fish stock and Burgundy wine.

Bring to a boil and simmer for 30 - 40 minutes.

Place all ingredients in a thick-bottomed pan with some more olive oil. Pour fish stock mixture in the pan and simmer for five to ten minutes.

Season to taste.

Serve with sourdough bread and sprinkle with remaining herbs.

Recommended Wines

Vichon 1990 Cabernet Sauvignon

Fetzer Barrel Select Sauvignon Blanc 1991

San Francisco Delta Salmon

Sour Cream Bernaise & Salmon Caviar

North America

Method

Marinate salmon in olive oil with salt and pepper for 2 hours.

Make Bernaise sauce. Finish and add sour cream and salmon caviar under Bernaise sauce.

Either sauté the marinated salmon fillets or grill.

Serve the salmon fillets with the sauce.

Garnish.

Recommended Wines

Fetzer Barrel Select Chardonnay 1991

Fetzer Barrel Select Cabernet Sauvignon 1991

Ingredients

Serves 4
4 pieces 7 oz salmon fillet
4 tsp olive oil
coarse salt
fresh ground pepper
2 Tbsp sour cream
2 Tbsp salmon caviar

Bernaise Sauce:
$^1/_2$ cup white wine
$^1/_2$ cup white wine vinegar
1 oz shallots, chopped
1 oz fresh tarragon, chopped
1 oz fresh chervil
3 egg yolks
6 oz butter
pinch of cayenne
lemon juice

Garnish:
baby carrots, blanched
asparagus spears
8 Tbsp salmon caviar
6 tsp green onions, chopped

Catalina Swordfish Steak

with Mission Fig Relish

North America

Ingredients

Serves 4
4 each 7-8 oz swordfish steaks
2 tsp rosemary
4 doves garlic, crushed
4 tsp oil

for Fig Relish:
36 ripe figs, peeled
6 tomatoes, skinned
3 small red onions
6 Jalapeno or Serrano peppers
4 oz tomato juice
1 oz cilantro, chopped
4 oz fig chutney

Garnish:
4 raw ripe figs, sliced thin
20 pieces snow peas
12 thin slices lemon

Method

Marinate swordfish with rosemary, garlic and oil.
Season with salt and pepper.

for Fig Relish:
Dice all ingredients fine, then mix together with fig chutney and tomato juice. Season to taste, allow to stand for at least two hours.
Grill or sauté the marinated swordfish.

Garnish:
Trim the snow peas to show ribbon edges, then sauté.

Recommended Wines

Robert Mondavi 1992 Chardonnay

Vichon 1990 Cabernet Sauvignon

Turkey Breast With Wild Mushrooms

North America

Method

Butterfly and flatten turkey breast to one centimeter. Season with salt and pepper, spread with mustard.

Peppercorn Sauce:

Place the following in a blender: turkey trimmings, thyme, cream, Madeira wine, lemon juice, salt and pepper. Blend.

Sauté mushrooms, parsley and shallots in a saucepan.

Place in ice cold bowl and fold all ingredients together.

Add mixture to center of flattened turkey breast. Roll and season.

Place on buttered aluminium foil, roll tight.

Roast slowly for 20 - 30 minutes at 150 degrees Celsius.

Slice and serve with the peppercorn sauce.

Garnish.

Recommended Wines

Fetzer Barrel Select Chardonnay 1991

Fetzer Barrel Select Sauvignon Blanc 1991

Ingredients

Serves 8

2 each 600 g Louis Rich turkey breast

3 Tbsp Grey Poupon Dijon mustard

250 g turkey breast trimmings

1 Tbsp lemon juice

60 ml Madeira wine

2 Tbsp thyme

2 Tbsp parsley

75 g wild mushrooms, sliced

2 shallots, chopped

250 ml 32% cream

salt

pepper

1 tsp butter

Garnish:

broad beans, blanched

baby carrots, blanched

whole wild mushrooms

sprigs of parsley

Turkey with Sun-dried Cranberry Sauce

North America

Method

Dissolve sugar in water and bring to caramel blend over medium heat.

Add apple cider vinegar and stir until dissolved.

In a separate saucepan, bring cranberries to boil in cranberry juice. Add to sugar mixture.

Add heated demiglaze and orange juice concentrate.

Season with salt and pepper to taste.

Garnish as shown.

Ingredients

Serves 4

4 each 3 oz Louis Rich turkey tenderloin medallions
1 cup water
1 cup sugar
³/₄ cup apple cider vinegar
6 oz sun-dried cranberries
6 oz cranberry juice
³/₄ oz demiglaze
¹/₈ cup orange juice concentrate
salt, pepper

Garnish:

orange sections, peeled carrots, finely julienne baby zucchinis

Recommended Wines

Robert Mondavi 1991 Pinot Noir

Fetzer Barrel Select Sauvignon Blanc 1991

Barony Pheasant Breast

with Dark Meat Ravioli Plum Demiglaze

North America

Ingredients

Serves 4
1 each whole pheasant
1 sheet ravioli dough
1 tsp shallots, diced
$^1/_2$ tsp rosemary leaves
4 oz demiglaze
2 oz plum coulis
2 oz white wine
2 oz butter, clarified
1 oz brandy

Garnish:
vegetables

Method

Remove breast from carcass leaving wing joints attached. Cut wings at first joint away from breast and french the bone. Set aside. Remove legs and thighs from carcass remove skin. Finely dice meat taken from legs and thighs.

Heat one ounce butter in sauté pan, add shallots and meat, sauté lightly for two to three minutes. Deglaze with white wine and add one ounce demiglaze. Season. Remove.

Lay out pasta dough and cut into four pieces. Brush two pieces with cool water and divide leg meat between the two. Place two remaining pieces on top of leg meat and seal edges. Cut ravioli to desired shape. Season the pheasant breast generously. Sauté breast on both sides in hot butter. Roast in oven to desired temperature.

Cook ravioli in boiling water; sauté lightly in butter and season with salt, pepper and fresh herbs.

Remove pheasant breast from oven. Allow to rest briefly. Place ravioli on plate and garnish.

Pour sauce on the plate. Slice the pheasant breast very thin and fan out on top of the sauce. Serve immediately.

for the Sauce:

Heat the basic plum coulis in a small pan. Add brandy and flame off alcohol. Add the rest of the demiglaze and reduce by a quarter.

Veal Chop Filled with French Brie

North America

Method

Make a cut in the side of the veal chop big enough to push frozen brie cheese into it. Season and sear in skillet and finish in 350 degrees Farenheit oven.

Prepare sauce as per recipe and assemble on plate with vegetables as shown.

Sun-dried Tomato Sauce:

In a saucepan, sauté sun-dried tomatoes and shallots and deglaze with brandy. Add chicken stock and bring to a boil. Mix butter and flour and blend into sauce until smooth, then add heavy cream and return to boil and simmer 20 minutes.

Finish the sauce with glace de viande and seasoning.

Recommended Wines

Robert Mondavi 1991 Pinot Noir

Fetzer Valley Oaks Cabernet Sauvignon 1990

Ingredients

Serves 4
4 veal chops 250 g each (bone on)
60 g brie cheese (freeze before use)
60 ml *sun-dried tomato sauce for veal
salt, pepper to taste

for Sun-dried Tomato Sauce:
50 g sundried tomato, julienne
50 g shallots, chopped
50 ml brandy
35 g butter
40 g flour
250 ml chicken stock
250 ml 35% cream
salt, pepper to taste

Garnish:
mixed vegetables, blanched
sprigs of rosemary
20 ml glace de viande

Grilled Smoked Lamb Loin

North America

Ingredients

Serves 2
2 loins of lamb
2 cups warm water
1 cup Kosher salt
¹/₄ cup granulated sugar
2 cups cool water
8 Tbsp olive oil
parchment paper

Method

Combine the warm water, Kosher salt and sugar in a stainless steel bowl, whisking until the salt and sugar have dissolved. Whisk in the cool water.

Place the lamb pieces in the brine for five minutes. Remove the lamb from the brine. Drain on paper towels, then refrigerate uncovered for one hour.

Line the center shelf of the smoker with parchment paper. Place the lamb on the parchment and smoke for one hour, turning the pieces over half hourly. Transfer the smoked lamb to a baking sheet and refrigerate, loosely covered with film wrap, until completely cool, about two hours.

Coat the smoked lamb with four tablespoons of olive oil, then season with salt and pepper. Grill the lamb over a hot charcoal fire for two to three minutes per side. Keep basting with olive oil.

Slice and garnish.

Recommended Wines

Fetzer Barrel Select Cabernet Sauvignon 1989

Fetzer Barrel Select Zinfandel 1989

American Lamb Loin Stuffed

with Leeks and Baked in Puff Pastry

North America

Method

Season lamb with salt and pepper, rub with minced garlic. Sear in a hot pan.

Stuff lamb loin with leeks, wrap in puff pastry and bake at 450 degrees Fahrenheit to the desired specification.

Reduce lamb jus over medium heat by half. Add chopped herbs, whisk in butter little at a time. Season to taste.

Slice lamb loin, place on a plate and garnish with desired vegetables.

Lace with lamb-herb sauce.

Sauté all vegetables for garnish.

Ingredients

Serves 1
1 American lamb loin
salt, pepper
1 clove garlic, minced
$^{1}/_{2}$ piece leek, blanched
puff pastry as required
1 cup lamb jus
1 tsp fresh rosemary and thyme, chopped
1 Tbsp butter

Garnish:
broad beans
broccoli tips
carrot rounds
white asparagus

Recommended Wines

Robert Mondavi 1991 Pinot Noir

Fetzer Barrel Select Cabernet Sauvignon 1989

Ruedi Blattler
Executive Chef
The Westin Harbor Castle, Toronto

The Westin Harbor Castle,
Toronto, Canada

A native Swiss, Chef Ruedi Blattler began his career in the famed Swiss resort of St. Moritz. Besides working in his homeland, Ruedi has worked abroad in Japan and Australia. In 1974 he came to Canada to work both in Calgary and Edmonton and then moved to Toronto and the Westin Harbour Castle in 1988.

Chef Blattler is very much a trendsetter rather than a follower and he has been well recognized for his sense of style and presentation.

The successful apprentice program under Ruedi's tutorship is an example of his enthusiasm to pass on his art to young Canadians and those committed to excellence. The vigorous three- year apprentice course at the hotel, is a successful example of Ruedi's determination and commitment to make Canadian culinarians proud leaders in his field.

Hazelnut Bundt Cake

North America

Method

In a mixer, mix the butter, sugar, salt. Switch off, add to the mixture, by hand, the eggs, pastry flour and baking powder.

Mix together the almond or hazelnut meal, rum and chocolate chips and add to above.

Put the mixture in a well greased large muffin tray and bake in a preheated over of 180 degrees Celsius until done. Cakes are done when, upon sticking a skewer in, skewer should pull out clean.

Note: Decorate plate with white and dark chocolate sauce, see page 73 for chocolate sauce recipe. Substitute dark chocolate with white chocolate where necessary, or vice versa.

Ingredients

Serves 10

3 lb 8 oz butter

3 lb 8 oz sugar

pinch salt

24 eggs

10 ¹/₂ oz rum

3 lb 8 oz pastry flour

1 ¹/₂ oz baking powder

2 lb almond meal or hazelnut meal

1 lb dark chocolate chips

1 lb white chocolate chips

Recommended Wines

Fetzer Gewürztraminer 1991

Bollinger Special Cuvee Champagne (Non-vintage)

Chocolate Mammoth

North America

Ingredients

Serves 10
1 lb 8 oz chocolate couverture
6 egg yolks
4 oz water
4 oz rum
6 oz egg white
4 oz sugar

Garnish:
raspberry coulis
1 qt whipping cream

Method

Melt chocolate couverture.

Whip and add to melted chocolate, the egg yolks, water and rum.

Separately, whip to snow, the egg white and sugar and add to above.

Fold into the above and set in a cooler to chill.

Garnish with raspberry coulis and whipping cream.

Recommended Wines

Fetzer Barrel Gewürztraminer 1991

Fetzer Barrel Select Cabernet Sauvignon 1989

Bread and Walnut Pudding

North America

Method

Separate the eggs and chill the whites. Whip the yolks together with sugar until white. Gradually add melted butter.

Grind walnuts, add to mixture.

Whip the whites until they stand in peaks.

Fold in the walnuts and chocoloate and transfer to an oiled soufflé dish which has been buttered and coated with the breadcrumbs.

Bake at 200 degrees Celsius for thirty minutes.

Garnish with kiwi fruit slices, vanilla sauce and raspberry coulis.

Ingredients

Serves 4

4 eggs

8 oz walnuts

1 oz butter, melted

2 Tbsp dry breadcrumbs

4 oz vanilla sauce

1 kiwi fruit, sliced

8 Tbsp raspberry coulis

4 oz sugar

4 oz chocolate

Recommended Wines

Fetzer Barrel Select Cabernet Sauvignon 1989

Fetzer Valley Oaks Cabernet Sauvignon 1990

Pumpkin Mousse

North America

Ingredients

Serves 8
8 sheets gelatine
4 cups vanilla sauce
1 lb Libby's pumpkin
4 egg yolks
3 oz sugar
pinch of allspice
pinch of nutmeg
pinch of cinnamon
pinch of salt
4 cups whipping cream

Method

Warm vanilla sauce and add to gelatin.

Grate pumpkin finely.

Add to above, the pumpkin, egg yolks, sugar, allspice, nutmeg, cinnamon and salt.

Fold the whipping cream into the above.

Let it cool overnight in the refrigerator.

Recommended Wines

Fetzer Gewürztraminer 1991

Bollinger Special Cuvee Champagne (Non-vintage)

Palo Alto Plum Pudding

North America

Method

Soak the dried fruits with Amaretto Di Saronno and rum for 48 hours.

Cream together butter, brown sugar, salt and spices using a low speed mixer with a paddle. Add beaten eggs slowly. Add molasses. Add soaked dried fruit to rum. Add orange and lemon peel. Add flour and breadcrumbs and mix until blended.

Line appropriate sized bowl with cheese cloth and put mixture in, leave room for expansion. Tie off cheese cloth and cover with foil. Steam for two to three hours.

When done, this will keep for several months and increase in flavor with time.

Serve with brandy butter or a sweet rum sauce.

Reheat by steam when needed and flambé with warm brandy.

Ingredients

Serves 4

8 oz butter
8 oz brown sugar
$1/8$ oz salt
$1/8$ oz allspice
$1/2$ oz powdered ginger
8 eggs
8 oz dark molasses
3 oz rum
3 oz Amaretto Di Saronno
8 oz bread flour
1 lb California raisins
1 lb currants
8 oz golden raisins
8 oz orange peel
4 oz lemon peel
8 oz breadcrumbs

Recommended Wines

Fetzer Gewürztraminer 1991

Fetzer Barrel Select Zinfandel 1989

Ceci all'Olio

(Golden Christmas Bread)

Italy

Method

Have handy a sheet of wax paper about nine inch square. Put filling ingredients into a large bowl, mix everything well using your hands. Divide the filling into four equal parts and gently form each one into a sort of a ball. Lay the finished balls on the wax paper for later use.

Divide your bread dough into four equal parts and gently roll them around with your hands to form balls. Roll each ball into a circle one sixteenth of an inch thick.

Put one fig ball in the center of each of the rolled dough pieces. Pick up the edges of the bread dough and bring them all together just above the center of the fig ball. Gently grasp them and twist them so that the resulting design looks like a swirl. This seals the bread and keeps the stuffing inside. Try not to make this part of the dough too thick. It should be as uniform as possible all round. Brush the loaves all over with the olive oil, not too much, just so they glisten.

Preheat the oven to 375 degrees Fahrenheit, place the loaves on a baking sheet, and let them rest in a warm place for as long as it takes your oven to attain the desired temperature.

Put the loaves in the middle of the oven and bake them for 30 minutes, or until the dough is a deep gold all over, including the bottom. Take them out of the oven to cool on a rack.

Ingredients

Serves 6
1 recipe basic bread dough made with olive oil, once risen
all purpose flour for rolling dough
virgin olive oil for brushing finished loaves

for filling:
1 lb dry black figs, ground medium fine
¹/₂ cup whole pinenuts, toasted
³/₄ cup whole hazelnuts, toasted
³/₄ cup almonds, toasted and chopped coarsely
2 Tbsp candied orange peel, finely chopped
¹/₃ cup apricot preserves

Swiss Grittibanz

Switzerland

Ingredients

Serves 6
6 cups all-purpose flour
¹/₄ package active dry yeast
¹/₃ cup sugar
1 ¹/₂ cups warm milk
¹/₃ cup butter, melted and cooled
2 eggs
1 tsp salt
grated peel of 1 lemon
2 egg yolks beaten with 1 tsp of water (for glaze)

Method

Preheat oven to 375 degrees Fahrenheit. Sift four cups of flour into bowl and make well in center. Place yeast and one tablespoon sugar in well. Add milk and stir to dissolve yeast. Sprinkle yeast mixture with flour. Cover bowl with clean towel and let stand ten minutes . Beat remaining sugar, butter, eggs, salt and lemon peel until blended. Add to bowl with one cup flour. Beat vigorously with wooden spoon until smooth. Stir in enough remaining flour to make smooth dough that comes away from side of bowl. Cover and let rise about one hour.

Grease baking sheets. Punch dough down and divide in half. Set one larger piece of dough aside. Divide remaining piece of dough into eight pieces: one large piece for the body, seven smaller pieces for the head, arms, legs, hat and trimmings. Flatten large piece of dough, shape body and place on prepared baking sheet. Brush with beaten egg yolk mixture. Shape head, arms, legs, hat and trimmings.

Attach parts to body with egg yolk mixture. Cover the finished figure and let rise for 20 minutes. Brush with egg yolk mixture for finish. Bake 30 - 35 minutes in moderate oven.

Stollen

Germany

Method

Mix lukewarm milk, yeast and one ounce bread flour into soupy dough and let rise for 30 minutes and set to side. Mix butter and sugar to a foamy dough, then add eggs and egg yolks slowly for approximately five minutes.

Sift flour, nutmeg and mace and add alternately with once ounce milk. Mix approximately two minutes.

Coat dried fruits, peel and slivered almonds with flour to avoid sticking and add to dough. Let dough rest for twenty minutes. Knead dough and wait another 20 minutes.

Flatten the loaf and fold in half. Place loaf on baking pan and bake at 350 degrees Fahrenheit for 40 - 45 minutes. Cool for ten minutes.

Brush with melted butter and roll in granulated sugar.

After completely cool, sift powdered sugar on top.

Ingredients

Serves 8
3 oz lukewarm milk
2 oz fresh yeast
1 oz bread flour
7 oz butter
4 oz granulated sugar
2 eggs
2 egg yolks
4 oz almonds, slivered
1 lb 7 oz bread flour
1 pinch nutmeg and mace
1 cup milk
3 oz currants
2 oz candied orange and lemon peel
1 oz melted butter
1 oz granulated sugar
sprinkle of powdered sugar

Mole de Platano

(Plantain Mole)

Latin America

Ingredients

Serves 4

4 plantains (bananas)
2 oz pumpkin seeds
1 oz sesame seeds
1 inch cinnamon stick, grounded
1 bar Mexican chocolate
3 white peppercorns, grounded
6 cloves, grounded
3 croissants
10 ripe tomatoes
1 chilli pasilla, seeded
1 piece achiote
4 oz lard
$^1/_2$ lb sugar
$^1/_2$ tsp salt

Method

Peel plantains and slice in round pieces. Fry in lard. Roast two ounces pumpkin seeds, one ounce sesame seeds, cinnamon, peppercorn, cloves. Toast the croissant separately. Cook ten tomatoes and one chilli pasilla in a saucepan with some lard.

Blend all the toasted ingredients; add the chocolate and small piece of achiote, adding the cooked tomatoes and chilli pasilla and the toasted croissants.

Fry everything in lard. Once the mixture thickens, add sugar and salt.

Add sliced plantains and cook for a few minutes.

To serve, top with sesame seeds.

Recommended Wines

Fetzer Barrel Select Cabernet Sauvignon 1989

Fetzer Gewürztraminer 1991

Arroz con Leche

(Rice with Milk)

Latin America, Guatemala

Method

Rinse rice and put in a saucepan, then add to it boiling water, cinnamon and salt. Keep cooking on high heat for three minutes. When rice is cooked, add milk and sugar. Cook for five minutes or until rice mixture thickens.

Serve in bowl, sprinkle with ground cinnamon and garnish with cinnamon stick.

Ingredients

Serves 4
100 g rice
500 ml boiling water
500 ml milk
¹/₂ stick cinnamon
100 g sugar
pinch salt
pinch of ground cinnamon

Recommended Wine

Fetzer Gewürztraminer 1991

Merry Christmas

Spiced Viennese Coffee

North America

Method

Make coffee with the instant or freeze dried coffee, combining sugar, spices and stir until dissolved.

Pour from one container or coffee pot to another to make sure you get a uniform brew.

Add the Amaretto Di Saronno and pour into demitasse cups.

Garnish with prepared whipped cream and serve with cinnamon sticks as stirrer.

Ingredients

Serves 6
1 l boiling water
40 g 97% caffeine free instant or freeze dried coffee
40 g sugar
1 Tbsp ground cinnamon
1 tsp ground cloves
whipped cream
1 cup Amaretto Di Saronno
6 cinnamon sticks

Creamy Coffee Royal

North America

Ingredients

Serves 2
12 fl oz hot brewed
Yuban coffee
1/2 tsp orange extract
2 scoops vanilla ice cream
grated nutmeg or cinnamon
2 fl oz orange and cognac brandy
liqueur (optional)

Method

Combine coffee, orange extract and liqueur in mugs.
Add scoops of ice cream.
Sprinkle with nutmeg or cinnamon.

Note: **May be served hot or cold, with or without liqueur.**

Coffee Rumba

North America

Method

Combine coffee with remaining ingredients in mugs.
Top with whipped topping, sprinkle with nutmeg and
garnish with maraschino cherry if desired.

Ingredients

Serves 2

*1 ¹/₂ cups double strength hot
brewed Maxwell House or Yuban
or Brim decaffeinated coffee*
2 fl oz coffee liqueur
1 fl oz C J Wray Dry Rum
4 Tbsp Half-and-Half

Coffee Carioca

North America

Ingredients

Serves 8
2 oranges, peeled
1 pouch Maxwell House, Brim,
Yuban decaffeinated coffee or
Sanka 97% caffeine free coffee
$^1/_4$ cup sugar
$^1/_2$ cup C J Wray Rum
whipped cream topping (optional)

Method

Remove peel from oranges in long quarter inch slices. Place in decanter of brewer. Brew coffee as directed.

Stir in sugar and rum.

Serve in regular or demitasse cups with whipped topping.

Garnish with orange rind strips or grated orange rind, shaved chocolate or ground cinnamon, if desired.

Coffee Grog

North America

Method

Cream butter with brown sugar; add spices and salt. Store in jar with tight fitting cover in refrigerator.

Makes one cup base, or enough for 16 servings.

For each serving, combine one tablespoon base with three tablespoons rum, two tablespoon heavy cream and a strip of lemon peel and orange peel in a mug; stir in two-thirds cup brewed coffee.

Ingredients

Serves 16
¹/₄ cup butter or margarine

Base:
2 cups firmly packed brown sugar
¹/₄ tsp each cinnamon, nutmeg, allspice and cloves
¹/₈ tsp salt

for serving:
C J Wray Dry Rum, as required
heavy cream, as required
strips of lemon and orange peel, as required
freshly brewed Maxwell House or Sanka 97% caffeine free coffee, as required

Coffee Islander

North America

Ingredients

Serves 2
C J Wray Dry Rum, as required
granulated sugar, as required
1 ½ cups hot brewed Maxwell
House or Yuban coffee
4 Tbsp coffee liqueur
2 Tbsp light C J Wray Dry Rum
orange slices

Method

Dip rims of heatproof glasses in rum, then dip in granulated sugar to coat evenly.

Add coffee, liqueur and one tablespoon C J Wray Dry Rum; stir gently.

Serve immediately.

Garnish with orange slices, if desired.

Almond Twilight

North America

Method

Combine coffee with brown sugar and liqueur in heat proof glass or mug.
Garnish with orange peel, if desired.

Ingredients

Serves 2

1 ½ cups double strength hot brewed Maxwell House, Yuban coffee, Brim decaffeinated coffee or Sanka 97% caffeine free coffee

1 Tbsp brown sugar

1 oz almond liqueur

Danish Coffee

North America

Method

Combine coffee, aromatic bitters and orange rind in demitasse cup.

Stir in liqueur.

Garnish with strips of orange rind, if desired.

Ingredients

Serves 2

1 cup single strength hot brewed Maxwell House or Yuban coffee or Sanka 97% caffeine free coffee

$^1/_2$ tsp aromatic bitters

2 oz grated orange rind

4 Tbsp dark Creme de Cacao liqueur

Westin
Hotels & Resorts

WORLDWIDE
(as at time of publication, January 1994)

CANADA

Calgary
Alberta
The Westin Hotel

Edmonton
Alberta
The Westin Hotel

Ottawa
Ontario
The Westin Hotel

Toronto
Ontario
The Westin Harbour Castle

Vancouver
British Columbia
The Westin Bayshore

Winnipeg
Manitoba
The Westin Hotel

MEXICO

Acapulco
Guerrero
Las Brisas

Cancún
Quintana Roo
The Westin Regina Resort

Ixtapa
Guerrero
The Westin Resort

MEXICO (continued)

México City
The Westin Galeria Plaza

**Puerto Vallarta
Jalisco**
The Westin Regina Resort

UNITED STATES OF AMERICA

**Atlanta
Georgia**
The Westin Peachtree Plaza

**Boston
Massachusetts**
*The Westin Hotel
Copley Place*

**Boston
Massachusetts**
*The Westin Hotel
Waltham*

**Chicago
Illinois**
The Westin Hotel

**Chicago
Illinois**
*The Westin Hotel
O'Hare*

**Cincinnati
Ohio**
The Westin Hotel

**Coral Gables
Florida - Miami area**
*The Biltmore Hotel
Coral Gables*

**Dallas
Texas**
*The Westin Hotel
Galleria*

**Denver
Colorado**
*The Westin Hotel
Tabor Center*

**Detroit
Michigan**
*The Westin Hotel
Renaissance Center*

**Fort Lauderdale
Florida**
*The Westin Hotel
Cypress Creek*

**Hilton Head Island
South Carolina**
The Westin Resort

**Houston
Texas**
The Westin Galleria

**Houston
Texas**
The Westin Oaks

**Indianapolis
Indiana**
The Westin Hotel

**Kansas City
Missouri**
The Westin Crown Center

**Kauai
Hawaii**
*The Westin Kauai
Kauai Lagoons*

**Los Angeles -Westside
California**
*Century Plaza Hotel
and Tower*

**Los Angeles
California**
The Westin Bonaventure

**Los Angeles
California**
*The Westin Hotel,
Los Angeles Airport*

**Maui
Hawaii**
*(Kaanapali Beach)
The Westin Maui*

**New Orleans
Louisiana**
The Westin Canal Place

**New York
New York**
The Algonquin

**New York
New York**
The Plaza

**Orange County
California**
*The Westin
South Coast Plaza*

**Orlando
Florida
Walt Disney World**
Walt Disney World Swan

**Phoenix
Arizona**
Arizona Biltmore

**Pittsburgh
Pennsylvania**
The Westin William Penn

UNITED STATES OF AMERICA (continued)

**Portland
Oregon**
Governor Hotel

**Rancho Mirage
California - Palm Springs**
*The Westin
Mission Hills Resort*

**San Francisco
California**
*The Westin Hotel
San Francisco Airport*

**San Francisco
California**
The Westin St. Francis

**Santa Clara
California**
The Westin Hotel

**Seattle
Washington**
The Westin Hotel

**Tucson
Arizona**
The Westin La Paloma

**Vail
Colorado**
The Westin Resort

Washington, D.C.
ANA Hotel

ARGENTINA   GUATEMALA

Buenos Aires
Caesar Park

**El Remate
Petén**
Camino Real Tikal

Guatemala City
Camino Real

BRAZIL

Fortaleza
Caesar Park

Rio de Janeiro
Caesar Park Ipanema

Sào Paulo
Caesar Park

Vitória
*Caesar Park Fazenda
Monte Verde*

CHINA

Shanghai
*The Westin Hotel
Shanghai*

KOREA

Pusan
The Westin Chosun Beach

Seoul
The Westin Chosun

MACAU

Coloane Ilha
The Westin Resort

MALAYSIA

Langkawi
The Mahsuri Westin Resort

PHILLIPINES

Manila
*The Westin
Philippine Plaza*

TAIWAN

Kenting
Caesar Park

THAILAND

Chiangmai
The Westin Chiangmai

SINGAPORE

**Singapore
Raffles City**
The Westin Plaza

**Singapore
Raffles City**
The Westin Stamford

236

JAPAN

Kyoto
The Miyako

Kyoto
The Westin Kyoto
Takara-ga-ike Prince Hotel

Osaka
The Westin Osaka

Tokyo
Hotel Grand Palace

Tokyo
Palace Hotel

GERMANY   # PORTUGAL

Hamburg
Hotel Vier Jahreszeiten

Sintra
Caesar Park Penha Longa

EGYPT

Hurghada
The Westin Palm Beach
Resort

The Photographers

To all the photographers of both food and hotel architecture (interior and exterior) who have contributed to this book; from all over the world, we extend our thank you.

Mark Knight & Nick Pira

Collectively known as "Southern Exposure", specializes in all aspects of Hotel and Resort Photography. With studios in the United Sates and Italy, they are especially adept and seasoned in the art of large-scale location photography assignments. They first became associated with this project two years ago, through Mr Kurt H Fischer and subsequently photographed more than 500 entrees, appetizers and desserts for the making of the book.

Alex Ortega

Alex Ortega is a creative and talented professional freelance photographer based in Asia. In the last few years, he has been involved in six exhibitions of his work, all of which received excellent reviews. Ortega is, in every way, an artist in his own right, putting images on film that captures one's imagination.

Craig Matthew of Matthew Photographic Services, Catabasas, for the group photograph of the Menu Development Task Force for "Spirit of the Season".

The Artists

We want to also thank the two artists who created the original promotion artwork reproduced at the beginning of each of the four parts in this book.

Yoko Sato Killion

Ms Yoko Sato Killion, the creator for the cover of "Seafood of the World". As it was an international promotion, the design also needed to have an international look, so she used rice paper for the background and a vertical title to give a look which is anything but American.

Gloria Chenoweth

Ms Chenoweth designed the promotion cover of "Spirit of the Season", "España" and "Spring is in the Air". A graphic designer and illustrator, who, in recent years has created images for Westin Hotels & Resorts' seasonal food and beverage promotions.

Menu Development Task Force

To all the personnel of Westin Hotels & Resorts around the world who have participated in the developing of recipes for all promotions in this book, we thank you.

The following appears in photographs in this book:

Rudolph (Ruedi) Blattler - *Executive Chef*	154, 210
Waldo Brun - *Corporate Executive Chef*	16, 50, 52, 76
Carlos Cancho - *Sous Chef*	50
Richard Carpenter - *Executive Pastry Chef*	50, 64
Kenny Chei - *Apprentice*	50
Thierry Dufour - *Executive Chef*	154
Marcus Dunbar - *Executive Chef*	76, 92
Lee Evans - *Corporate Procurement Manager*	76
Kurt H Fischer - *Vice President, Food & Beverage*	9, 16, 50, 76, 154
Edward Gee - *Assistant Pastry Chef*	50
Werner Glur - *Executive Chef*	154, 168
Christopher Guinn - *Sous Chef*	76
Hans Günter Harms - *Chef de Cuisine*	76, 146
Mark Hellbach - *Executive Chef*	76, 116
Menze Heroian - *Director, Food & Beverage*	50
Patrick Honeywell - *Pastry Chef*	16
Roberto Iglesias - *Executive Chef*	154, 162
Minao Ishizaka - *Executive Chef*	76, 98
Tadashi Katoh - *Chef de Cuisine*	76, 110, 154
Andreas Knapp- *Former Executive Chef*	154
Christoph Leu - *Executive Chef*	16, 28
Bernd Liebergesell - *Executive Chef*	186
Ulrich Ludwig - *Executive Chef*	16, 34
Fabiano Marcolini - *Executive Chef*	76
David S Milligan - *Vice President*	50
Jamie Morningstar - *Chef*	76
David O' Connor - *Master Sommelier*	128
Manfred Ochs - *Executive Chef*	154, 180
Tylun Pang - *Executive Chef*	16, 18, 154
Michael Quinttus - *Vice President*	76
Jose Ramon - *Executive Chef*	50
David C Roveto - *Vice President*	154
Daniel Simard - *Executive Chef*	16, 38
Kimberley Storey - *Apprentice*	50
Felix Subuyuj-Buccaro - *Chef de Cuisine*	154
Otto Weibel - *Director of Kitchens*	1, 198
Bryan S Wilson - *Winemaker*	16
Gerhardt Wind - *Executive Chef*	154, 174
Heinz Zasche - *Executive Pastry Chef*	76, 86

Wines

Kurt H. Fischer
Vice President, Food & Beverage

1991 Barrel Select Chardonnay
Barrel-fermented and barrel-aged. Creamy-vanilla, light-butterscotch aromas with pineapple and apple-spice flavors.

1989 Fetzer Barrel Select Cabernet Sauvignon
A toasty-oak, spicy aroma is an enticing prelude to complex flavors of cherries layered by undertones of mint, clove and cedar. Delicious, lingering chocolate and cherry finish. Medium tannins.

1991 Fetzer Barrel Select Sauvignon Blanc
Classic Sauvignon Blanc character with a mildly grassy-citrus nose followed by melons and figs. Citrus and toasty oak-spice complexity provide a crisp, clean finish.

1990 Fetzer Barrel Select Zinfandel
Complex aromas of blackberry, cherry, and spice co-mingle with well-balanced berry-peppery flavors and a spicy finish.

1990 Fetzer Valley Oaks Cabernet Sauvignon
A quintessential North Coast Cabernet with rich, earth aromas followed by smooth flavors of black cherries, raspberries and cedar. Oak aging and medium tannins contribute to an accessible, balanced wine.

1991 Fetzer Gewürztraminer
A classic California style Gewürztraminer with complex varietal characteristics. The wine has aromas of jasmine followed by flavors of pears and apples; a complex, spicy finish lingers in the mouth.

1991 Sonoma County Chardonnay
Has a brillant light bold hue. Its tropical and citrus aromas are reminiscent of pineapple, mango, kiwi and mandarin orange, combined with creamy vanilla and clove accents from fermentation and aging in French oak barrels. The abundantly rich flavors are crisp and tightly structured. The balance of fruit and toasty oak flavors presents a long and pleasing finish.

1990 Sonoma County Cabernet Sauvignon
Bright garnet in color, it has aromas that are likened to cassis, blackberry and cranberry, with herbal minty notes. The aromas carry through to flavors, with the addition of bright Bing cherry and hints of vanilla. Forward and packed with fruit, it balanced with firm acidity and restrained tannins. Its approachable character provided an toasty warm finish.

1991 Sonoma County Pinot Blanc
Its ripe fruit flavors of pineapple and apple combine with butterscotch, coconut cream, roasted hazelnuts, toast and vanilla, flavor combinations achieved through painstaking malolactic fermentation, barrel fermentation, and aging in French oak barrels. This is a wine meant for savoring with a meal or just sipping casually.

1991 Sonoma County Fumé Blanc
This Fumé Blanc should be enjoyed within three years of its vintage date when its fresh fruit flavors are at their peak. Accompanies fresh, succulent seafood - oysters on the half-shell, baked halibut, cracked crab, broiled shrimp or grilled snapper. It is also a fine companion to simple chicken dishes.

1990 Sonoma County Merlot
The hallmark of this wine is fruit: sweet, floral aromas of cherries and cranberries dominate. Rich oak-spice, black pepper, and slight cedar notes are also present. Intense flavors of cranberry, oak, clove-spice and orange fill the mouth and linger in the soft finish.

1992 Sonoma County Muscat Canelli
It has aromas of pink grapefruit, peaches and pineapple mingle with the citrus notes of orange blossom, tangerines and mandarin oranges. These aromas carry through to the flavors, augmented with accents of exotic nectar and cinnamon sticks. It is a clean, refreshing dessert wine, highlights which are seldom found in other sweet wines.

1988 Sonoma County Blanc de Blancs
Benziger proudly introduces an elegant "Methode Champenoise" Blanc de Blancs sparkling wine from the 1988 vintage. Made from 100% Chardonnay grapes, it is uniquely compatible with a wide range of cuisines. Fesh and delicate, this sparkler can be enjoyed not only as an aperitif, but it will complement a variety of entrees and desserts.

Christian Moueix 1988 Merlot
The name Moueix has for the better part of this century been the most authoritative presence in Pomerol and Saint-Emilion, appellations where the Merlot vine is dominant. Christian Moueix Merlot is the first varietal wine to bear the name of the dynamic man behind the recent brilliance of Ets. Jean-Pierre Moueix.

Cape Mentelle Shiraz 1989, Margaret River, Southwest Australia
Heady green pepper and spice typify the Cape Mentelle Shiraz, mellow and rich with a soft supple palate.

1991 Vichon Napa Valley Chevrignon
The wine combines light tropical fruit and spearmint notes with a crisp, long finish, making "Chev" ideal for service with a wide variety of foods (although it's pretty good on it sown, as well). We like it with shellfish and other seafood, but we also serve it with the spicy foods of China, Thailand, the Southwest, and of course, Cajun country. Enjoy!

1991 Vichon Napa Valley Chardonnay
Oak. Sur-lie aging, combined with regular stirring of the lees, contributed Depth, complexity and richness to this wine. Crisp lemon and tropical fruit aromas and flavors are complemented by the creamy, rich mouthfeel.

1990 Vichon Napa Valley Cabernet Sauvignon
This is loaded with rich varietal fruit flavors – blackberry and black cherry are the most prominent – and undertones of black pepper and toasty oak are spicy complements. This is a velvety smooth Cabernet with a long, satisfying finish. Roasted leg of lamb, grilled sirloin strip, hearty pasta dishes and aged cheeses are some of the foods we enjoy most with this wine.

1986 Gran Coronas
Elegant Cabernet fruit on nose. Well developed and mature.

Gran Viña Sol
Fuller flavored, Chardonnay character, with a hint of vanilla from oak aging.

1985 Gran Coronas Mas La Plana
100% Cabernet Sauvignon, specially selected from Torres' finest vineyard. Complex, with fine fruit flavors and velvety finish.

Viña Sol
Fresh and crisp with intense fruit. Ideal with seafood or chicken

Sangre De Toro
Full flavored, spicy with a hint of raspberry.

1982 Gran Sangre De Toro
Deep ruby color, intense aroma, rich in flavor with a soft round finish.

1990 Deinhard Riesling Dry
From the banks of the Rhine, the finest Riesling grapes are harvested to produce this wine -
an exciting new concept for German wines.
Deinhard uses the classic Riesling grape to produce a wine that develops in the bottle, a
wine with a delicate flowery nose, elegant dryness and perfect balance.
Try Deinhard Riesling Dry as the perfect alternative to Chardonnay.

1983 Bernkasteler Doctor Riesling
The Bernkasteler Doctor is without doubt Germany's most famous vineyard, often referred
to as "the Romanee Conti of Germany". The Doctor complements most desserts.

Robert Mondavi Woodbridge 1991 Sauvignon Blanc
This wine is a great complement to a variety of foods; try it with a zesty lemon
pasta, shellfish or grilled seafood.

Robert Mondavi Woodbridge 1992 Chardonnay
The 1991 Woodbridge Chardonnay is a great choice with grilled fish or chicken
and a variety of pasta dishes.

Robert Mondavi 1991 Pinot Noir
Our 1990 Pinot Noir is a wine of great finesse. Subtle spice aromas and flavors
complement forward cherry fruit flavors and undertones of oak and vanilla.
Complex and harmonious, this exceptional wine possesses a long, silky finish.

Robert Mondavi 1990 Fumé Blanc
This is a rich, full Fume Blanc of great balance and finesse. It has concentrated
floral and apricot aromas and slightly spicy varietal flavors. Complementing the
flintiness of the Sauvignon Blanc, the semillon fruit adds round, supple qualities to
the wine.

Robert Mondavi 1991 Chardonnay Reserve
Is an elegant wine of great balance and finesse. Bright, fruity flavors — primarily
apple and light citrus — are complemented by vanilla and oak undertones. A rich,
harmonious wine, the 1991 Chardonnay possesses a long, smooth finish.

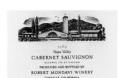

Robert Mondavi 1989 Cabernet Sauvignon
The 1989 Robert Mondavi Cabernet Sauvignon is a wine of intense aromas —
primarily black cherry, cedar and spice — and complex flavors; oak undertones
complement the more pronounced plum fruit and spice flavors. An extremely
approachable wine with full, forward fruit, enjoy it now with your favorite foods.

Corporate Support

Westin Hotels & Resorts Corporate Headquarters, Seattle, Washington USA, would like to extend a special thank you to the following corporations and suppliers to their hotels around the world; who have helped in their various ways, encouraged and supported the publication of this first book in a series to be published *"FOOD & WINE THE WESTIN WAY"*.

Page 8

The Homer Laughlin China Company

Page 44

General Foods USA

Page 80

Robert Mondavi Winery

Page 122

Hiram Walker & Sons Inc

Page 192

Fetzer Winery

 **Benziger Glen Ellen Wines**

 **Ore-Cal Corp**
Harvest of the Sea

 **Knott's Berry Farm Foods**

 Oscar Mayer Foods

 **The Paddington Corporation**
representing Amaretto Di Saronno

 **Remy Amerique Inc**
representing Cointreau Liqueur

 **The House of Seagram**
representing Mumm Cuvee Napa

 **Uncle Ben's**

 Washington State Apple Commission

Glossary

achiote	Seeds of the annatto, or a preparation made from them, used to flavor various foods.
aïoli	A mayonnaise-type sauce made with egg yolks, garlic and olive oil.
Aji-no-moto	Monosodium glutamate, a flavoring widely used in Asian cooking.
al dente	A description of the consistency of pasta that is best for taste.
allspice	Flavored by a mixture of cinnamon, cloves and nutmeg.
Amaretto Di Saronno	An Italian apricot liqueur.
antipasto	An Italian term for a selection of hot or cold food served as an appetizer.
Arugula	A green leafy vegetable with distinctive flavor, most often used in salads and garnishes.
Bacalao	Salted cod fillets.
bain-marie	A French description of a low-sided container which is half filled with water of just below boiling point. Used for keeping inner container with food placed in them warm. Sometimes also referred to as a double saucepan.
basil	A herb with a distinctive, pungent taste usually used in salads.
beignet	Fritters.
Belgian endive	*see* chicory.
bell pepper	sweet pepper
bisque	A rich creamy soup made from a thick purée of seafood, game or vegetables.
blanching	Food immersed in boiling water to whiten it or cook.
blend	To mix to a smooth paste, usually with added liquid in the preparation of soups or sauces.
blini	A small thick savory pancake made with a leavened batter that contains both wheat flour and buckwheat flour.
Bonito	A name given to various species of oily sea fish found in the Oceans.
Boucheé	A bite-sized round piece of cooked puff pastry served hot with savory filling on top or inside.
bouillon	A plain, unclarified meat/vegetable stock that is strained, flavored and served as soup or as base for sauces; stock.
bouquet garni	A small bunch of herbs tied together and used to give flavor to stews, soups, stocks. Usually consists of sprigs of parsley, thyme, bay leaf, cloves and peppercorn. Can be wrapped in muslin. Commercial bouquet garni can be found in most supermarkets.

Brie	A soft textured cheese with a floury crust but soft all through. Available at supermarkets.
brioche	An enriched yeast dough baked in the shape of a cottage loaf; can have savory or sweet fillings in them.
broil	Grill.
broiler	As in "broiler chicken"- chicken weighing from one and one-half to two and one-half pounds, or cooking method - to grill.
brunoise	A mixture of finely diced or shredded vegetables used as a soup or sauce base, can also be used as a garnish.
burdock	A green leafy weed with purple leaves and roots used in cooking.
button mushrooms	Champignons.
caramel	"Burnt" sugar. A syrupy substance obtained by heating sugar slowly until a rich brown color.
chantilly	A sweetened version of whipped cream which can be flavored with vanilla or brandy.
chervil	A herb with a sweet delicate flavor.
chicory	can be spelt chiccore, chiccory - a pear-shaped vegetable with white fleshy leaves. It is the same family as Frisee - a curly-leaved dark green lettuce. Raddicio is another type of chicory, but reddish in color. All these can be used in salads.
chilli poblanos	Poblano chilli pepper.
chilli pepper	A small but spicy hot variety of the pepper family. Can be bought in whole dried form, in sauce, flakes or powder form.
Chinese cabbage	A type of Asian cabbage that looks like a long lettuce, known also as Bak Choy or Pak Choy.
choux past	Choux pastry, a sweet or savoury dough often used to make croquembouches - filled or iced to make desserts or hors d'oeuvres.
chutney	A thick piquant sauce/purée of fruits or vegetables, usually served as a condiment.
cilantro	A herb used as a condiment, also known as Chinese parsley or coriander.
cocote	A cooking pot with lid, a casserole dish. This can also be used to describe small soufflé dishes.
cominos	Caraway.
compote	A dish of fresh or dried fruit stewed in sugar syrup, can be made from one fruit or a mixture of fruits. Can also be flavored with spices, lemon, orange or wine. Is also a name given to stew made from game birds where the meat is cooked until very tender.
condiment	A name used for strongly flavored sauces, relishes, vinegars, salt, pepper, which are served at the table as an accompaniment to other foods.

confit	A French name for a preserve usually made with duck, goose, pork portions. Usually cooked for a long time to seal the meats in their own juices.
consommé	A concentrated and clarified stock, made by boiling strained beef, poultry, veal stock and reduce until concentrated.
coriander	*see* cilantro.
cornichon	Small pickle.
couverture	Raw chocolate.
crepe	Thin pancakes, can be served plain or with savory mixture.
croquettes	A cooked mixture of fish, meat or vegetables held together with beaten egg or thick sauce and formed into round rolls.
croutons	Small pieces of bread, toasted or fried, served as an accompaniment to soups or in salads.
cumin	A spice related to parsley, similar to caraway.
Daikon	A kind of radish, widely cultivated as a vegetable in the Far East, also called Japanese radish or Satsuma radish. Also known as 'mooli'.
Dandelion	A wild plant considered a weed, now popular as a vegetable. When picking dandelion leaves, make sure they are in a clean area and pick the leaves before the flower heads develop.
deglaze	The adding of liquid to a pan that had food roasted in, to either make a sauce or gravy with the sedimented food left in the pan.
demiglaze	A rich classic French brown sauce, sherry or Madiera can be added to flavor it.
dende oil	A yellowish fatty oil used in making chocolate; palm oil.
diamond	Taditional form , shape or cut usually of vegetables.
dice	To cut food into small cubes.
dl	deciliter, *see* Conversion Tables.
eggplant	Aubergine.
eggwash	A mixture of egg yolk and water used to brush over dough before baking. Gives baked goods a shiny shell.
epazote	Mexican tea, wormseed. This is a strong flavored herb used in Mexican cooking and can be used as a tea.
farcé	Forcemeat or stuffing.
fennel	There are two types of this: the fine leaved one is a herb while the other, which has a bulb-type root can be eaten as a vegetable.
fish fumé	Fish broth; stock.
fish velouté	A basic white sauce made with stock, thickened with a white or golden roux.
French bread	A baguette, crustry long bread.

ginkonut	The oval pale-green fruit of the Asian ginko tree; much used in Japanese cooking, either roasted or grilled, as a garnish for fish or poultry or simply as a dessert nut.
glace de viande	Removing all fat from a stock by boiling and straining until substance coats the back of a spoon.
glass noodles	Vermicelli, or rice sticks.
gravlax	A famous Swedish dish made by dry-salting raw salmon fillets. Usually served thinly sliced as an appetizer.
green onions	Also known as spring onions or in some places, scallions. Popular with stir fried dishes in Chinese cooking or used as garnish.
ground meat	Minced meat
Haricot verts	Also known as French beans and snap beans.
hominy	A whole dried corn without the yellow husk. Before use, it has to be softened either by boiling in milk or water.
hominy	Corn soaked and ground; boiled like porridge.
horseradish	A member of the mustard family.
Jicama	Tuberous root vegetable, most often julienne and served in salads.
jujube	An oval olive-sized fruit with a smooth tough red skin, soft sweet yellowish or green flesh, and a hard stone.
julienne	Cut into very fine strips of equal lengths.
jus	Natural juice or gravy of meat.
Kale	A member of the cabbage family.
Kosher	A name used to describe food cooked according to Jewish law.
Langoustine	French name for scampi, a crustacean related to the lobster.
lard	Fat obtained from pig, which has been melted down.
laurel	Bayleaf used as seasoning in cooking.
Lollo Rosso	A type of lettuce with frilly leaves.
mache	Can be spelt Marche, also known as lamb's lettuce, a small leaved winter plant which is not a true lettuce.
Madiera	A fortified wine named after the Portuguese island where it is made.
mirepoix	A culinary preparation created in the 18th century, used to enhance the flavor of meat, game and fish; in the preparation of sauces and as a garnish. Also a French name for a mixture of cut vegetables.
mirin	Japanese sweet wine, usually used in cooking.
mis de pain	White breadcrumbs.
miso shiro	Bean paste made from fermented soya beans, popular in Japanese cookery.
morels	A very tasty but rare mushroom.

Nicoise	French term used to describe dishes made or garnished with either tomatoes or cucumbers, French beans, black olives, parsley or basil.
Nori	Seaweed.
pate de sucre	Sweetened paste.
Pernod	A bitter liqueur.
pesto	A paste, not strained.
pimiento	Pimiento, Spanish name for a variety of red or green sweet peppers.
pinenuts	Small, pale cream-colored seed of a tree from the Meditterannean.
Plantains	A variety of banana mainly used in cooking.
pompadum	Poppadom, pompadoums, are one of the same. It is a savory Indian biscuit, very thin, very light and crisp.
pumpkin seeds	These large flat, green seeds can be eaten raw or cooked in sweet or savory dishes.
purée	Food that has been pounded, sieved or liquidized, usually after cooking, to give a smooth fine pulp.
Quahog	Also known as "Littleneck" or "hardshell" clams.
Quail	A small game bird.
Quinoa	Not a true cereal grain, but can be used in a similar way. Leaves can be used for salad; seeds used in soup and in making beer.
Raddicio	Can be spelt raddichio - *see* chicory.
reduce	To fast boil a liquid in an uncovered pan in order to evaporate surplus liquid and give a more concentrated result.
roux	A mixture of fat and flour cooked to form the basis of a sauce.
sabayon	A French term to describe a light frothy consistency.
saffron	Most expensive of spices, it comes from the stigmas of the saffron plant. It originates from Spain.
sake	A Japanese wine, made from fermented rice.
salsa	Condiment or sauce made of chopped fresh vegetables. Italian or Spanish term applied to a variety of international sauces.
sauté	To cook food in fat to brown it lightly.
scallions	*see* green onions.
shiso	Mixed Japanese cresse.
sorbeitiére	An electric appliance used to make ice creams and sorbets.
soya sauce	Soy sauce, shoyu all refers to a light or dark brown salty sauce made from soya beans.
squab	Young pigeon.
strudel	Wafer-thin pastry rolled around a sweet or savoury filling.
sweat	Cooking food, usually vegetables in oil or melted fat until the juices run.

Szechuan pepper	Hot aromatic spice made from dried berries of a Chinese tree, can also mean dried spicy hot peppers.
tapas	In Spain, an assortment of hors d'oeuvres or cocktail snacks which can sometimes take the place of dinner.
Timbale	A round mould with straight or sloping sides made of heatproof China or tinned copper.
tomatillos	Small green tomatoes.
turned	A special cut of vegetables or potatoes.
Udon	Japanese noodles with a narrow ribbon-like appearance, white in color.
wasabi	Japanese horseradish.
Zucchini	Courgette.

Index